INTRODUCTION

HAVE YOU EVER SEEN A SAND DUNE?

When I was a child, my family occasionally vacationed in the Outer Banks of North Carolina. One of the major attractions in that area is called Jockey's Ridge. Jockey's Ridge is a series of enormous sand dunes so tall that you can see both the ocean and the sound while standing atop them.

As a child, we would run down the dunes as fast as we could, sometimes picking up incredible speed, sometimes leaping and soaring through the air, and sometimes tumbling down the dunes so badly that many of us are still shaking sand out of our ears.

One time, though, we found something strange as we reached the base of the dunes. Out of the sand sprouted forth a flag. We tried to remove the flag, but it wouldn't budge. So we started digging.

As we dug, we realized that the sand was actually part of a castle. The castle was huge. The more we dug into the sand, the more castle appeared. We couldn't figure out why this castle was here until we reached the bottom.

At the base of the castle was green artificial turf. And just off to the side was a hole.

The castle was part of a miniature golf course!

Decades earlier, the sand dunes had shifted and covered an entire miniature golf course. What once was clearly visible eventually became obscured and lost.

This is the problem that many of us face when we try to read the Bible. I know that it was for me.

For many of us, it can feel like the Bible is buried in sand. While, no doubt, the Holy Spirit can speak to us through God's word, we often feel like we're missing something. So much of the context, history, and culture has been lost over the centuries. We know that there is so much more, but we don't know what it is or where to begin.

Some of us feel as if the flag sticking above the sand is all we can ever see. Others of us have caught a glimpse of the castle. But what we really long for is to see the full picture of what lies beneath the layers, to truly understand what happened, and what it means for our lives.

1

I felt this way for a long time. For much of my life, the Bible made little more sense than a flag sticking out of the sand. Then, one day, I found a book that changed everything. The book was called "Sitting at the Feet of Rabbi Jesus" by Ann Spangler and Lois Tverberg.

It was through this book that I was introduced to the world of first-century Israel. I began to learn exactly what it meant that Jesus was a rabbi. I began to understand how the geography mentioned in the Bible was critical to understanding the story. And I began to learn how understanding the broader and deeper meanings of words could change the meaning of an entire passage.

Once I began to move *Beyond the Words* to truly study and wrestle with the context, history, culture, and language of scripture, I began to see the Bible with an entirely new set of eyes.

I felt like I was there, like I could see the scriptures unfolding before me! I noticed small details that challenged my assumptions and myths about scripture. And best of all, I uncovered lessons that had hitherto gone unnoticed.

Let me give you an example:

Every nativity scene I have ever seen has depicted three magi visiting the baby Jesus.

But here's the thing: this is not the scene we witness in scripture.

Not only does scripture never say that there were three magi (see Day 16), but it also never says that Jesus was a baby when they arrived.

In koine Greek, *brephos* is the word for an infant or newborn. This is the word Luke uses in Luke 2:16 to describe Jesus as he lays in the manger. It's the same word used to describe John the Baptist when he leaps inside of Elizabeth's womb.

But Matthew, whose gospel recounts the arrival of the magi, doesn't use *brephos*; he uses *paidion*. *Paidion* is the Greek word for a young child.

Paidion is also the word Matthew uses to describe Jesus when his family returns from Egypt. It is the term he uses when he says Jesus fed 5,000 men, plus women and children. It is the word he uses when Jesus tells a young girl who is dead to stand up. And it is the word he uses when people bring children to Jesus and the disciples try to shoo them away.

Every time, Matthew uses *paidion*, not *brephos*.

Now it's easy to see how we assumed Jesus was still an infant. The story of the magi immediately follows the mention of Jesus' birth. But it's only when we begin to look beyond our English words, beyond the stories we've seen depicted on stage and television throughout our lives, that we begin to get a clear picture.

Anyone reading or listening to this passage in the first century would have known exactly what Matthew was saying when he used the word *paidion*. They would have been like the people who played on the miniature golf course before it was covered in sand.

But not us. Our view is obscured. Our English translations don't convey this subtle difference. And it is only once we move *Beyond the Words* that the full picture begins to become clear.

This devotional is intended to help you begin to see the fuller picture of scripture. The words you study each day will help you sweep away layers of sand to see what lies beneath.

EACH DAY, I will introduce you to a word that will alter how you interpret key Bible passages. I will help you understand the context and history impacting its translation and broader meaning. Then, I will list other scriptures that include that word, including instances where a Greek word is used to replace a Hebrew word Jesus would have spoken, so that you might see how this new understanding impacts your interpretation of those passages.

IN SOME CASES, when I suggest a verse in order to highlight an alternate meaning of a word, it may be difficult to locate that word in your English translation. I recommend using a resource like BlueLetterBible.org to view the original language and locate the relevant word. This will allow you to see where the original word falls in the sentence and how it has been translated.

FINALLY, each day, I will also give you questions to consider that will help you apply these insights to your relationship with Jesus.

My hope is that these will be 30 days that change the way you read the Bible. May you not only gain insight into the words shared within this book; may God also instill in you a hunger to know more. May you begin to picture the world of Jesus in your mind, understand scriptures in entirely new ways, and grow closer to the Lord than ever before!

I'M SO GRATEFUL TO HAVE YOU JOIN ME ON THIS JOURNEY OVER THE NEXT 30 DAYS! SO LET'S DIVE IN AND BEGIN EXPLORING TOGETHER WHAT LIES *BEYOND THE WORDS*...

TABLE OF CONTENTS

DAY 1

YADA

YAW-DAH'

ידע

"I will give them a heart to *know* me, that I am the LORD. They will be my people, and I will be their God, for they will return to me with all their heart."

Jeremiah 24:7

Do I know you?

Have you ever asked someone that question? Perhaps you saw them in a checkout line or from across the street. Something about them seemed familiar. You thought you might have met them before.

Or maybe it was something they said – their accent or the way they phrased something. It seemed familiar, reminded you of something from your past that you couldn't quite place.

Or it could be that it was just your favorite pick-up line in your 20s! ...even though it never worked.

But in the end, the question was always the same: do I know you?

Do I know you?

There is a lot wrapped up in that word "know," isn't there?

What does it mean to know someone? Do I know someone simply because I know something about them? Even something as simple as their name? Or does knowledge reflect something more personal?

Consider this verse from the Psalms…

"**THOSE WHO KNOW YOUR NAME TRUST IN YOU, FOR YOU, LORD, HAVE NEVER FORSAKEN THOSE WHO SEEK YOU**"

PSALM 9:10

The author of this Psalm isn't simply saying that everyone who has heard the name *Yahweh* will automatically trust in the Lord. If this were the case, Israel would have been freed from centuries of violence since those invading nations, upon hearing God's name, would have turned from their idols and put their faith in the Lord.

No, there is something more going on here.

You see, the Hebrew word that we translate as "know" is the word *yada*. But *yada* doesn't simply refer to knowledge in terms of the information we have accumulated in our minds. That isn't how Hebrew people thought.

Yada refers to knowledge that has come through a relationship. The Psalmist is saying that those who *know* God's name will trust God because their knowledge stems from the relationship they have with God. What they know, what they understand about God, has come from their experiences with God, the moments God has been faithful to them in the past, and the works they have seen God do.

It's easy to gather information about God. But it's something entirely different to know God.

One is a distant perspective on an impersonal being.
The other is truly a relationship.

So, ask yourself.....

What is the difference between learning about Jesus by watching a television show like "The Chosen" and truly knowing Jesus?

_____
_____
_____
_____
_____
_____
_____

Do you feel like you know information about God? Or do you truly know God through a relationship with God?

_____
_____
_____
_____
_____
_____
_____

Was there a moment in your life where you felt like you went from knowing about God to truly having a relationship with Jesus?

_____
_____
_____
_____
_____
_____
_____

What steps can you take each day to deepen your relationship with the Lord?

_____
_____
_____
_____

RELATED SCRIPTURES TO STUDY

EXODUS 1:8   ISAIAH 12:5   EZEKIEL 20:39-44

SHEMA

SHEH'-MAH

שמע

"*Hear*, O Israel, the Lord is our God, the Lord is one. You shall love the Lord your God with all your heart and with all your soul and with all your strength."

Deuteronomy 6:4-5

The other morning, I went into my daughter's room to wake her up. This is a new thing for me, given that, only a few months ago, she was waking me up at 4 AM! Nevertheless, since she now can sleep well into the morning, I tried my best to wake her, using a variety of tactics.

I kissed her forehead.
I nudged her shoulder.
I set up a small griddle so she could wake up to the smell of crackling bacon.

....but nothing worked.

Then I noticed something: she was smiling. It was ever so slight, but it was there. In the corner of her mouth, there was the faintest grin. She could hear me, but she wasn't responding.

I wonder if God feels the same way about us sometimes?

One of the most important Hebrew words anyone should know is the word *shema*. It is a word that Jesus said every single day because it was part of an essential prayer in Jewish life.

Each day, people of the Jewish faith would quote the words of Deuteronomy:

> "HEAR, O ISRAEL, THE LORD IS OUR GOD, THE LORD IS ONE. YOU SHALL LOVE THE LORD YOUR GOD WITH ALL YOUR HEART AND WITH ALL YOUR SOUL AND WITH ALL YOUR STRENGTH"
> DEUTERONOMY 6:4-5

Jesus himself said that this was the greatest of all of the commands in scripture. It is foundational to our relationship with God.

And the very first word in this passage....is *shema*.

Shema is the Hebrew word that means "to hear." But its meaning goes beyond that.

Shema also means "to obey."

You see, in Hebrew, words don't only describe action; they also describe outcome. *Shema* is meant not only to describe the act of hearing but the result of that action: obedience.

And when you understand this, all of a sudden, other scriptures begin to come alive – like when Jesus says, "Whoever has ears to hear, let them hear" (Matthew 11:15).

Jesus doesn't want people to just hear the words he's saying. He wants them to obey.

God's desire isn't for us to simply read the Bible and memorize the words. God's desire is for us to act.

So, as you're reading scripture, every time you hear God say "listen" or "hear," God is also saying "obey." God is calling us to action.

Our mission in this world is to make disciples, to spread the Good News of Jesus to the ends of the earth. And this Great Commission cannot be accomplished merely through reading books and memorizing Bible verses.

The Kingdom of God cannot grow when all we do is listen.

We must move. We must act. We must obey.

What are some areas in your life where you are "hearing" Jesus but not obeying?

_____

_____

What are some steps you can take toward obedience?

_____

_____

What are obstacles that are getting in the way?

_____

_____

Who in your life can help you to overcome these obstacles?

_____

_____

Challenge: Search scripture for the words "listen" and "hear" and see how this deeper meaning of *shema* changes the way you understand those passages.

_____

_____

RELATED SCRIPTURES TO STUDY

GENESIS 27:8   ISAIAH 1:10   MARK 4:9

AGAPE

AG-AH'-PAY

ἀγάπη

"*Love* is patient, *love* is kind. It does not envy, it does not boast, it is not proud. It does not dishonor others, it is not self-seeking, it is not easily angered, it keeps no record of wrongs. *Love* does not delight in evil but rejoices with the truth. It always protects, always trusts, always hopes, always perseveres."

1 Corinthians 13:4–7

I have had the privilege of performing a lot of wedding ceremonies over the years. Many pastors try to avoid weddings, but I actually like them. There is so much joy, so much love, and so many delicious appetizers!

One of the first things I have couples do in our premarital sessions is select the scriptures for their ceremony. I try to make it clear from the very beginning that the focus of our time together isn't so much going to be on the wedding itself but on everything that happens after. I want to ensure that they don't spend months (or even years) preparing for a wedding and little to no time preparing for the rest of their lives together. The scripture they choose will be a significant part of the wedding ceremony and impact our premarital sessions.

More often than not, I can predict exactly what passage couples are going to choose. It's not going to be a sultry passage from Song of Solomon, or 1 John's discourse on love, or an apocalyptic disaster from Revelation illlustrating their fear of marriage (though this might have happened once or twice!).

Inevitably, most couples will choose the ever-familiar, always ubiquitous words of 1 Corinthians 13…

"LOVE IS PATIENT, LOVE IS KIND. IT DOES NOT ENVY, IT DOES NOT BOAST, IT IS NOT PROUD. IT DOES NOT DISHONOR OTHERS, IT IS NOT SELF-SEEKING, IT IS NOT EASILY ANGERED, IT KEEPS NO RECORD OF

WRONGS. LOVE DOES NOT DELIGHT IN EVIL BUT REJOICES WITH THE TRUTH. IT ALWAYS PROTECTS, ALWAYS TRUSTS, ALWAYS HOPES, ALWAYS PERSEVERES"

1 CORINTHIANS 13:4-7

Can I tell you a secret? I don't like this passage.

Well, that's not entirely true. I love the passage itself. I just really don't like it for weddings.

When couples approach marriage, everything is about romance, feelings of love, and attraction to one another. And, naturally, these feelings are imposed upon the words of 1 Corinthians 13. It becomes a passage on how to express romantic love.

But that's not at all what the passage is about….

1 Corinthians 13 is written to a church in turmoil. There is infighting. There is sin. And Paul is telling them how to love one another as the body of Christ.

You see, the word that Paul is using in these verses is the Greek word *agape*. *Agape* is a form of love used very intentionally in scripture. It is almost always used as a description of God's love for us and how God intends for us to love one another.

Perhaps a verse that really communicates the meaning of this word comes from another one of Paul's letters. Paul says,

"HUSBANDS, LOVE [*AGAPE*] YOUR WIVES, JUST AS CHRIST LOVED THE CHURCH AND GAVE HIMSELF UP FOR HER"

EPHESIANS 5:25

Throughout the New Testament, *agape* is connected to Christ. We love one another as Christ loved us. This love isn't just a romantic love or a friendly love; it's a sacrificial love. To love someone with *agape* is to be willing to lay down your life for them as Christ laid down his life for us.

So, maybe, in the end, 1 Corinthians 13 can be used to guide couples in their marriage – but not for the reasons we would think. Our love isn't patient, kind, and selfless because our romantic feelings compel it to be. Feelings change over time.

Instead, we demonstrate this form of love not just out of dedication to that other person but out of dedication to Christ. Our love for our spouse and so many others in our life is a reflection of both the love Jesus has for us and the love we strive to have for him.

Who in your life needs to experience *agape*? What are some ways in which you can demonstrate that love to them?

_____
_____
_____
_____

How would things change in churches today if people started reflecting *agape* love?

_____
_____
_____
_____

Search for the various uses of *agape* in scripture. How does an understanding of this word impact your understanding of these passages?

_____
_____
_____
_____

RELATED SCRIPTURES TO STUDY

JOHN 15:13   2 CORINTHIANS 5:14   1 JOHN 4:8

LEV

LAYV
לב

"I will give thanks to you, Lord, with all my *heart*; I will tell of all your wonderful deeds."

Psalm 9:1

Have you ever tried learning to play a musical instrument? When I was in college, I tried to learn the guitar. I love music and thought that it would be a lot of fun to be able to play the songs I enjoy.

And it didn't hurt that guys who play guitar are always surrounded by crowds of girls – at least, that's what I thought in college.

So, one day, I borrowed my grandfather's guitar and began to learn. I studied a book on chords. I purchased a few accessories to ensure my guitar was in tune and in good shape. And for several weeks, I practiced every day.

But I realized something: learning the guitar isn't easy. And I wasn't naturally gifted. So, eventually, I lost interest, and I just gave up.

I didn't have the heart for it.

Do you know what I mean? Most likely, you do.

I use that phrase "didn't have the heart for it" very intentionally. It's a phrase that's common in English. And it has a very specific meaning. To not have the "heart" for something means that you lack passion. You lack desire or emotion. These are things we associate with the heart.

So it's natural that we would assume these same beliefs are true when reading scripture. When we read about someone loving God with all their heart or having their hearts hardened, we assume that this reflects their passions, desires, and emotions.

…And we assume incorrectly.

This is one of the greatest challenges when reading the Bible. Sometimes there are cultural meanings attached to words that are quite different from our own.

In Hebrew, the word for "heart" is *lev*. But in Hebrew culture, *lev* isn't the seat of one's emotions. It's the source of one's thoughts.

This changes how we read many scriptures. For instance, when Jesus says to "love the Lord your God with all your heart…" (Matthew 22:37), he's not saying that we should feel strong emotions for God. He's saying that we should love God with every one of our thoughts. Our love for God should guide our thoughts and impact how we see the world.

The same is true for Psalm 9:1. When the Psalmist says,

> ## "I WILL GIVE THANKS TO YOU, LORD, WITH ALL MY HEART; I WILL TELL OF ALL YOUR WONDERFUL DEEDS"

he is saying that he will set his mind to giving thanks. It will impact the way he thinks, the way he sees the world.

This gives a whole new perspective to the idea of putting your "heart" into something – especially your relationship with God. While we can't necessarily manufacture our feelings, we can often control our thoughts. We can decide where we want to focus our attention; we can train our minds through habits and patterns.

And this can have a significant impact on our love for God!

How does an understanding of the word *lev* impact your understanding of what it means to love God with all of your heart?	What are some ways that you can begin to love God with all of your thoughts?	Who can help you with this?
_____	_____	_____
_____	_____	_____
_____	_____	_____
_____	_____	_____
_____	_____	_____
_____	_____	_____
_____	_____	_____
_____	_____	_____
_____	_____	_____
_____	_____	_____

RELATED SCRIPTURES TO STUDY

EXODUS 4:21   PROVERBS 12:25   MATTHEW 6:21

DAY 5

NEPHESH

NEH'-FESH

נֶפֶשׁ

"If they return to you with all of their heart and with all of their *soul* in the land of their enemies who took them captive and they pray to you toward their land which you gave to their ancestors, the city that you have chosen and the house that you built for your name, then you shall hear in heaven, the place of your dwelling, their prayer and their plea, and you shall vindicate them."

1 Kings 8:48-49

SOUL

When I was 11 years old, my great-grandmother passed away. This was one of my first experiences with death. I remember going to the funeral home the night before the funeral. I saw her lying in the casket. I witnessed my family members grieving. I discovered a plate of Oreos and consoled myself with chocolate cookies and "doublestuff" filling.

And then the next day, I was very sick. I'm not sure if it resulted from my Oreo binge or simply a stomach virus. Either way, I couldn't attend the funeral.

For those who did, though, they experienced something strange. At the end of the funeral, everyone said that a wind rushed through the crowd. The trees didn't move. Leaves didn't dance. It was only felt by the people present.

Everyone said that they felt like the "soul" of my grandmother had visited them in that moment.

That's what I tend to think of when I think of the "soul." The soul is a spirit separate from our bodies. It's the part of us that lives on after our mortal bodies have passed away.

But that isn't at all what Jesus thought when he thought of the soul. For the Hebrew people, the soul wasn't something that lived beyond this life. It was something quite active in this life.

For example, in 1 Kings, Solomon is in the midst of dedicating the newly built temple to the Lord. But while this is a glorious moment for the Israelite people, Solomon is not blinded by his success. He is aware of the story of Israel and their past struggles. He knows that when they have been faithful to God, they have prospered; but when they have turned their hearts away from God, they have suffered greatly.

So, as Solomon is praying over the temple, he addresses a situation in which Israel has suffered for its infidelity and says,

"IF THEY RETURN TO YOU WITH ALL OF THEIR HEART AND WITH ALL OF THEIR SOUL IN THE LAND OF THEIR ENEMIES WHO TOOK THEM CAPTIVE AND THEY PRAY TO YOU TOWARD THEIR LAND WHICH YOU GAVE TO THEIR ANCESTORS, THE CITY THAT YOU HAVE CHOSEN AND THE

HOUSE THAT YOU BUILT FOR YOUR NAME, THEN YOU SHALL HEAR IN HEAVEN, THE PLACE OF YOUR DWELLING, THEIR PRAYER AND THEIR PLEA, AND YOU SHALL VINDICATE THEM"
1 KINGS 8:48-49

Notice that word "soul." It is by returning to God with their "soul" that they are redeemed from the terrible situation in which they find themselves.

This isn't something separate from their body. It isn't something that will happen after their life on earth is over. It is something very current.

You see, the Hebrew word that Solomon is using here is *nephesh*. But *nephesh* isn't speaking of a spirit that lives within us and beyond us. In Hebrew, *nephesh* refers to a person's entire life.

The soul is every aspect of your life. Think of an athlete who is training to be the best at their sport. They commit every part of their lives to this task. Every action they undertake and every decision they make is centered around this commitment to be the very best. It consumes their entire lives.

This is what it means to love God with all of your soul. You don't give an hour to God on Sunday. You don't consider a daily quiet time to be "enough." When you love God with your entire soul, you love God in every area, with every action, every single day.

How does an understanding of the word *nephesh* change your understanding of the "soul"?	What would it look like for you to love God with all of your soul?	What steps can you begin to take today? Who can help you with this?

RELATED SCRIPTURES TO STUDY

1 KINGS 8:48   PSALM 116:7   JEREMIAH 6:16

M'EOD

MEH-ODE'

מאד

"Love the Lord your God with all your heart and with all your soul and with all your *strength*."

Deuteronomy 6:5

ENGLISH TRANSLATION

STRENGTH

06 | M'EOD

We don't get snow very often. If we are lucky, it will snow once or twice a winter.

Because of this, my youngest daughter doesn't really remember snow. She's seen pictures of past snow days. But she has no true memory of playing in the snow.

…until recently, that is.

This year, we got a big snow: 6 inches!

Naturally, my oldest daughter was excited to play with her friends in the snow. And my youngest did everything she could to keep up. She made snow angels, built a snowman, and picked off smaller children in a massive snowball fight.

It was pure winter bliss.

But after a few hours in the snow, my youngest daughter came into the house and collapsed on the couch. She was exhausted. We brought her some hot cocoa and a blanket. But before we had a chance to deliver them to her, she had fallen fast asleep.

She had given it her all outside, and now she had nothing left.

Do you know that feeling? It reminds me of an often-misunderstood word in scripture.

22

In Deuteronomy, we read,

> # "LOVE THE LORD YOUR GOD WITH ALL YOUR HEART AND WITH ALL YOUR SOUL AND WITH ALL YOUR STRENGTH"
> DEUTERONOMY 6:5

Jesus refers to this as the greatest of all commandments. However, as you've seen in previous chapters, it's a statement that's often misunderstood. Heart is a reference to our mind and thoughts. Soul is a reference to our entire life. And even the word for strength means something different than what we naturally assume.

The Hebrew word translated "strength" is the word *m'eod*. But *m'eod* doesn't actually mean strength. It literally means "very." The people are commanded to love God with all of their "very."

Another way of translating this term would be to say "with all of your 'oomph.'" *M'eod* means to love God with every ounce of energy that you have.

You can see why it is translated strength. But you can probably also see why that's not an entirely accurate translation.

We aren't commanded just to love God with the resources of our muscles. We are commanded to love God with the same passion and commitment that my daughter gave to the snow. We hold nothing back. We love God to the very last drop of strength we have.

The Deuteronomy passage makes it clear that the commitment God desires from us is immense. We are to love God with every one of our thoughts, every part of our lives, and with every ounce of our energy.

Our love for God is to be complete and consuming. This is the first and greatest of all commandments. This is the command upon which all other commandments rest.

Does this mean we have to be perfect? No. Of course not.

But it does mean that we must rethink what it means to be a disciple of Jesus. We must realize that this isn't something we relegate to a few hours or activities a week.

This is who we are. This is what defines us.

When it comes to our relationship with Jesus, we hold nothing back.

Is it possible that you have reduced your relationship with God to a few hours and activities a week? How so?

_____

_____

_____

_____

_____

What would it look like to love God with every ounce of energy you have?

_____

_____

_____

_____

_____

Where do you feel like you are doing this already?

_____

_____

_____

_____

_____

Who can help you as you strive to love God with all your *m'eod*?

_____

_____

_____

_____

_____

RELATED SCRIPTURES TO STUDY

1 SAMUEL 28:20

AVAD

AW-VAD
עבד

"Let my people go so they
may *worship* me."

Exodus 8:1

There is a moment in season 1, episode 2 of The Chosen, where Matthew is speaking to the Roman praetor Quintus. Repeatedly throughout the scene, Matthew refers to Quintus as "Dominus." It is a word that means "master" or "lord." In fact, it is the same word that slaves would use to refer to their owners.

It is a term suggesting complete subservience. At times, it even suggests worship.

Interestingly enough, there is a word in Hebrew that echoes this same connection between service and worship. It is the word *avad*.

Avad is a word that is typically translated "to serve." We see this when Jacob has worked for his uncle Laban for 14 years and asks to finally be able to leave with his family. He says,

"GIVE ME MY WIVES AND CHILDREN, FOR WHOM I HAVE SERVED YOU, AND I WILL BE ON MY WAY. YOU KNOW HOW MUCH WORK I'VE DONE FOR YOU"

GENESIS 30:26

In this case, *avad* simply means to work for someone; to do what they ask.

But in other instances, the meaning is deeper. For example, when the Israelites are slaves in Egypt, God tells pharaoh to

"LET MY PEOPLE GO SO THEY MAY WORSHIP ME"

EXODUS 8:1

The word translated "worship" is, once again, *avad*.

Remember, in Hebrew, words don't simply describe an action; they also describe the outcome of that action. We don't serve God simply to perform a task or accomplish a goal. God has a deeper desire: God desires our worship.

On the other hand, viewed from another perspective, we can also see that this teaches us something about worship.

Worship isn't a passive act in a big room. It is more than singing songs and listening to a sermon. Worship involves action. It requires that we surrender ourselves as servants of God.

Indeed, this may even change the way we view one of the 10 Commandments.

The fourth commandments says,

"SIX DAYS YOU SHALL LABOR [*AVAD*] AND DO ALL YOUR WORK, BUT THE SEVENTH DAY IS A SABBATH TO THE LORD YOUR GOD"
EXODUS 20:9-10

In other words, the way this command is written, it may be read to say that six days out of our week should be spent on *avad* – worshiping God. And on the 7th day, we rest.

This flips our whole week upside down. Too often, we think of worship as a day or as an event. But seen this way, God is actually commanding the opposite.

We should be worshiping God throughout our entire week. Every day, our worship should take the form of service, building God's Kingdom and furthering the gospel.

And one day a week, we rest from that.

This doesn't mean that we cease to worship God on that day. But we rest from our labor. We rest from the hard work of building the kingdom and we receive the gift of rest.

In the end, this is what it looks like for Jesus to be our "Dominus." He isn't someone we worship once a week or serve on occasion. Our entire lives are devoted to worshiping and serving him – the two are connected. This is the life of *avad*.

How has knowing the meaning of the word *avad* changed your understanding of what it means to worship Jesus? How has it changed the way you understand what it means to serve him?

_____

_____

_____

_____

_____

What are some ways you can restructure your life so you don't worship God once a week and rest the other six, but, instead, do the opposite?

_____

_____

_____

_____

_____

What are some opportunities for *avad* (opportunities to worship and serve God) that God has placed in your life?

_____

_____

_____

_____

_____

RELATED SCRIPTURES TO STUDY

JOSHUA 24:31   **JOB 21:15**   **JEREMIAH 5:19**

KAYEM & VATEL

KAH-YIM & VAH-TEL

בטל | קיים

"Do not think that I have come to *abolish* the Law or the Prophets; I have not come to abolish them but to *fulfill* them."

Matthew 5:17

29

FULFILL & ABOLISH

Should Christians read the Old Testament?

This is a question I wrestled with a lot as a child. One the one hand, there were many fascinating stories in the Old Testament: David and Goliath, Adam and Eve, Samson and Delilah.

But there were also a lot of things that confused me about the Old Testament. For instance, why does it say that we can't eat bacon? Why can't cheese go on a burger? And when it says that children are to be killed for disobedience, are they serious, or is that just an extreme parenting tactic?

I have known many people who have basically abandoned the Old Testament. They said to themselves, "All I need is Jesus anyway."

But is that true?

How do we grapple with the fact that Jesus studied the Old Testament and quoted it constantly throughout his ministry?

Well, there is one particular moment that brings much clarity to this dilemma. It's a phrase that confuses us in English, but made complete sense to Jesus' Hebrew audience.

In the midst of his Sermon on the Mount, Jesus says:

> "DO NOT THINK THAT I HAVE COME TO ABOLISH THE LAW OR THE PROPHETS; I HAVE NOT COME TO ABOLISH THEM BUT TO FULFILL THEM"
> MATTHEW 5:17

This is his opening sermon, the moment where he is establishing who he is and why he has come. He's declaring something very bold about his view of the Torah.

But what does he mean? What exactly is Jesus talking about when he says that he hasn't come to abolish the law, but to fulfill it?

Well, in order for this to make sense, we first have to understand a few idioms.

Kayem Torah are the Hebrew words translated "fulfilling the law." This was an idiom that meant to properly interpret the law. When rabbis agreed with one another on an interpretation of the law, they would say that each had "fulfilled" the law.

Kayem is a word that doesn't appear in scripture, but appears several times in the Mishnah, often used in the same way Jesus uses it in Matthew 5:17. For instance, a second-century rabbi named Rabbi Jonathan is recorded as saying,

"WHOEVER FULFILLS [KAYEM] THE TORAH WHILE IN A STATE OF POVERTY WILL ULTIMATELY FULFILL IT WHILE IN A STATE OF WEALTH; AND WHOEVER DISCARDS THE TORAH WHILE IN A STATE OF WEALTH WILL ULTIMATELY DISCARD IT WHILE IN A STATE OF POVERTY"*
MISHNAH PIRKEI AVOT 4:9

Rabbi Jonathan is saying that those who properly interpret the law when they are poor will also do so when they are wealthy. Compare this to the idea that a person who tithes when they are poor is more likely to tithe when they become wealthy. Their obedience in poverty becomes obedience in prosperity.

But there is another word I want you to notice. The word that is translated "discards" is the Hebrew word *vatel*. It can also mean to cease or abolish. Like *kayem*, *vatel* is used as an idiom. To "abolish the Torah" means to improperly interpret the Torah.

When you look closely at the ideas these idioms suggest, you begin to see why such strong language is used. If someone improperly interprets the Torah, they are stripping it of its meaning. They are leading people to sin and harming the community. It is as if the Torah did not exist or had been discarded entirely. Its benefit is lost.

At the same time, if someone properly interprets the Torah, they have helped others to live it out. The purpose and meaning of the Torah has come to life. What God intended through the law has been fulfilled.

So, when Jesus says that he has come not to abolish the Torah, but to fulfill it, he is claiming something about himself. He is declaring that he interprets the law correctly. While other religious leaders may believe he is leading people astray, Jesus wants them to know that he offers a perspective that is not only new but true.

Jesus is the Word made flesh. All of scripture has been fulfilled and brought to light in him. In truth, he is the only one who can fulfill the Torah and interpret it correctly, because he is its author.

Jesus never intended for us to discard the Old Testament teachings once he arrived. He intended for us to study them to apply them, but to do so with him as the lens through which we interpret them. For it is only through Jesus that we will ever truly understand God's word.

How does this change your understanding of Jesus' statement that he doesn't come to abolish the law, but fulfill it?

_____

_____

_____

_____

_____

Can you think of moments in scripture where Jesus "fulfills" the law by challenging the way religious leaders have been interpreting scripture?

_____

_____

_____

_____

_____

Have there been moments when God showed you that you were "abolishing" scripture by misinterpreting it? In what ways did God show you how to "fulfill" it by interpreting it differently?

_____

_____

_____

_____

_____

RELATED SCRIPTURES TO STUDY

MARK 7:10-13

*The Mishnah is a collection of Jewish oral traditions.

LECH ACHARAI

LEKH'AKH-AR-AHEE

לך אחרי

"As Jesus walked beside the Sea of Galilee, he saw Simon and his brother Andrew casting a net into the lake, for they were fishermen. "Come, *follow me*," Jesus said, "and I will send you out to fish for people." At once they left their nets and followed him."

Mark 1:16-17

When I was in college, I had a campus minister who would eventually become one of my lifelong mentors. He was a gifted preacher with an incredible ability to connect with young people. But what impacted me the most were the moments he would take me aside and impart a necessary piece of wisdom that immediately resolved some struggle in my life.

I remember one particular instance in which I was struggling with a situation involving a close friend. My friend was making very bad decisions that were harming him, and I didn't know how to respond. One day, I went to this campus minister and shared with him my dilemma. I'll never forget the words he said…

"Follow me."

This had almost become like a code word in our relationship. Whenever he would say this phrase, I knew to prepare myself for challenging questions or a profound insight.

I think of this mentor often when I read the gospels because, frequently throughout the gospels, we see Jesus use that exact same phrase: follow me.

It's easy to read those words and simply assume that Jesus wants people to walk alongside him or travel somewhere. But there is so much more wrapped up in that phrase.

You see, whenever a rabbi would call a young man to be his disciple, he would say two words: *lech acharai*. This is a Hebrew phrase that means "follow me." But in saying these words, a rabbi was inviting this man into a very close relationship. It meant that this young man would study under this rabbi.

But not everyone heard the words *lech acharai*. In fact, to hear these words was an incredible honor, reserved for only the most gifted of young men. Most men never studied under a rabbi. Instead, they would continue their family trade.

This is precisely what Simon Peter and Andrew were doing when Jesus approached them for the first time. They were fishing, just like their father before them. At some point in their lives, they had been told that they were not fit to study under a rabbi. This honor was not to be theirs.

So, imagine their surprise when Jesus approaches and says,

"COME, FOLLOW ME...AND I WILL SEND YOU OUT TO FISH FOR PEOPLE"

MARK 1:17

It's no wonder that they jump out of their boat – something critical to their livelihood and survival – and run to Jesus.

This offers us a whole new perspective on what it means for us to be disciples of Jesus. Being Jesus' disciples doesn't simply mean that we are students and Jesus is our teacher. That is one aspect of it; but there's more.

To be Jesus' disciple is an incredible honor. He is inviting us to follow him, to learn from him, to devote our lives to him, and most importantly, to be part of the incredible work he is doing to bring God's Kingdom here to earth.

The invitation is always before us. The question is: How will we choose to follow him today?

How has this insight into the phrase *lech acharai* impacted the way you view the story of the calling of Simon Peter and Andrew?

_____
_____
_____
_____
_____
_____

What do you think it means to be a disciple of Jesus?

_____
_____
_____
_____
_____
_____

Are there ever times when you don't feel good enough to be Jesus' disciple? Does it help to know that Jesus' first disciples felt that way too?

_____
_____
_____
_____
_____
_____

What is one thing you know that you need to do to follow Jesus today?

_____
_____

RELATED SCRIPTURES TO STUDY

MATTHEW 9:9   LUKE 18:18-30

RHABBI

HRAB-BEE'

ῥαββί

"Turning around, Jesus saw them
following and asked, 'What do you
want?' They said, 'Rabbi' (which
means "Teacher"), 'where are
you staying?'"

John 1:38

ENGLISH TRANSLATION
TEACHER

My favorite subject in high school was Latin.

(And, in case you're wondering why I didn't ever have a girlfriend in high school, see previous sentence.)

But the reason that Latin was my favorite subject wasn't necessarily because I loved the language. I mean, I did enjoy seeing connections between Latin words and English words and creating juvenile translations like "semper ubi sub ubi" ("always where under where"). But the real reason I loved Latin was because of my teacher.

My Latin teacher made class fun. She was interesting and engaging. She opened my eyes to the ancient Roman world and how a language that so many describe as "dead" is still alive today.

I find that when most people see the word *rhabbi* in scripture, which is often translated "rabbi" or "teacher," they imagine someone like my Latin teacher. They think of a person who instructs in a classroom. The teacher imparts knowledge and the students receive it.

But this isn't really what *rhabbi* means. Yes, a rabbi did teach. But the relationship between a rabbi and his disciples (students) was much different than our relationships with teachers today.

For one, as we saw in the case of Simon Peter and Andrew, not everyone could study under a rabbi. Only a select group were given this privilege. This is because the rabbi didn't just instruct through formalized lessons. Much of what the rabbi taught was through example. For a rabbi, learning wasn't simply a matter of the mind; it involved one's entire life.

A rabbi wasn't merely passing on spiritual information. A rabbi saw his role as leading his students along a path that would allow them to truly worship and serve God. And worshiping and serving God wasn't merely a career choice or a weekly event. It was all-consuming.

So, a rabbi would teach through everything he did: the way he tied his sandals, the way he prayed, the manner in which he covered his bald spot (ok, maybe not that one, but who knows?).

When we understand this, it tells us something about what it means for Jesus to be our rabbi. We aren't meant to solely focus on Jesus' words when we read scripture. This definitely isn't what Jesus' disciples did. Instead, we must focus on everything that Jesus does: how he interacts with people, where he takes his disciples, those subtle details that are easy to overlook but often speak volumes.

As disciples of Jesus, we want to know everything about our *rhabbi*. We don't just want to learn from him, we want to be like him in every way possible.

In the end, Jesus isn't just our teacher. He isn't just some wonderful moral guide. He is our Savior, our Lord. And every act of our lives should be focused on becoming more and more like him.

How has this insight into the role of rabbi changed the way you understand Jesus' relationship with his disciples?

_____
_____
_____
_____
_____
_____
_____
_____
_____
_____

How does this change what your relationship with Jesus should look like?

_____
_____
_____
_____
_____
_____
_____
_____
_____
_____

Challenge: Read through a chapter in the gospels and pay close attention to Jesus' actions. What does this teach you about how you should act as a follower of Jesus?

_____
_____
_____
_____
_____
_____
_____
_____

RELATED SCRIPTURES TO STUDY

MATTHEW 23:1-12   JOHN 3:2

MATHETES

MATH-AY-TES'

μαθητής

"Therefore, go and make *disciples* of all nations, baptizing them in the name of the Father, and of the Son, and of the Holy Spirit, teaching them to obey everything I have commanded you."

Matthew 28:19-20

When I was in college, a man came to our campus every year to preach just outside the main dining hall.

I say preach, but really, it was more like eight straight hours of yelling. I don't remember if he ever said anything about Jesus. All I remember was that everyone who walked past was doomed for hell.

One time, I even saw him point to the president of the Fellowship of Christian Athletes and declare that she was a fornicator and that she would spend eternity in Satan's clutches.

(I'm pretty sure she'd never even dated a boy, let alone done anything close to what he was saying.)

For much of my life, this was my image of evangelism. This was the image that came to mind when pastors and campus ministers would challenge us to live out the Great Commission:

> "THEREFORE, GO AND MAKE DISCIPLES OF ALL NATIONS, BAPTIZING THEM IN THE NAME OF THE FATHER, AND OF THE SON, AND OF THE HOLY SPIRIT, TEACHING THEM TO OBEY EVERYTHING I HAVE COMMANDED YOU"
>
> MATTHEW 28:19-20

Based on the behavior of the man on campus, Jesus' final command was that we go out and boldly tell people why they were destined for hell in hopes that they would repent.

Have you ever had an experience like this?

Thankfully, when I started to truly look at scripture, I realized that Jesus wasn't telling us to do anything remotely close to this. This wasn't at all what he meant when he said to "make disciples."

RELATED SCRIPTURE TO ST

ISAIAH 31:4   ISAIAH 38:14

So what did he mean?

Well, the word for a disciple that we see most commonly throughout scripture is the Greek word *mathetes*. It is a word that can also be translated "student." Today, we tend to think of a student as someone who absorbs information from a teacher. But discipleship went much further than that.

The reason a rabbi would say *lech acharai* (follow me) to a young man he was inviting to be his disciple, and the reason Simon Peter and Andrew jump out of their boat when Jesus says these words to them, is because discipling under a rabbi was a completely immersive experience.

Disciples would leave everything to follow their rabbi:

Their families....
Their businesses....
Their communities....
Everything!

They would go wherever the rabbi went and do whatever the rabbi did. A disciple's goal wasn't simply to learn what his rabbi knew. A disciple wanted to be just like his rabbi.

This is why Jesus said,

"IF ANYONE COMES TO ME AND DOES NOT HATE FATHER AND MOTHER, WIFE AND CHILDREN, BROTHERS AND SISTERS—YES, EVEN THEIR OWN LIFE—SUCH A PERSON CANNOT BE MY DISCIPLE"
LUKE 14:26

A disciple was willing to surrender everything in order to follow his rabbi. It was even said that the relationship between a rabbi and a disciple was closer than that of a disciple and his own father.

This is the kind of devotion we are to have in our relationship with Jesus. Jesus wants us to hold nothing back, to surrender every part of our lives to him.

Jesus doesn't just want us to know what he knows; he wants us to do what he did.

And just as importantly, Jesus is commanding us to help others do the same. The mission of the Kingdom of God is for every person to follow Jesus, to worship him as Savior and Lord and be his disciple.

And just imagine if we did this, if we were willing to follow Jesus as his disciples did, if we spread the Good News about him as they did?

How might our world be different? How might lives be changed? And how pleased might Jesus be that the ministry he began with those original disciples continues to grow through us today?

Having heard what it meant to be a disciple of Jesus, do you feel you have this kind of relationship with Jesus today?

_____

_____

_____

Have you surrendered every part of your life to Jesus?

_____

_____

_____

Is your primary mission in life to be like Jesus? What is holding you back?

_____

_____

_____

Who in your life can disciple you to be more like Jesus?

_____

_____

_____

Who can you disciple and help to grow in their relationship with Jesus?

_____

_____

_____

RELATED SCRIPTURES TO STUDY

MATTHEW 13:52   ACTS 14:21

TORAH

TO-RAW'

תורה

"Do not think that I have come to
abolish the *Law* or the Prophets;
I have not come to abolish them
but to fulfill them."

Matthew 5:17

When I was a teenager, I thanked my parents for all of their rules.

I gave them cards saying, "Thank you for not letting me be on the phone after 9PM." I would inscribe, "Thank you for requiring me to make my bed each morning." I would regale my friends with stories of how my parents wouldn't let me go to parties where there was underage drinking, prohibited me from spending all of my money on baseball cards, and made me eat my vegetables before I could have dessert.

I loved their rules!

And if you believe that, I've got a few million acres in the meta-verse to sell you (because, apparently, that's a thing now!).

Seriously, though, if you found what I just said incredible, you're absolutely right.

I didn't love rules growing up. Sometimes it seems like it's in our very nature to resist rules. We would be incredulous if someone claimed they loved a life bound by rules and restrictions,

…which is going to make what I'm about to tell you very surprising.

Because the truth is: the Jewish people did feel this way!

Every year, there were three festivals for which all Jewish people were required to travel to Jerusalem to worship at the temple.

One was Passover, the celebration of when God freed the Israelite people from slavery in Egypt.

Another was called Sukkot. This festival celebrated how God provided for the Israelite people while they traveled through the wilderness for forty years.

And finally, there was Shavuot. Shavuot marked the end of the barley harvest around seven weeks after Passover. But, at the time of Jesus, Shavuot also celebrated something else. Shavuot was the celebration of when God gave the law to Moses: 613 commandments detailing how the Israelite people should live.

Jewish people had an entire festival dedicated to celebrating the law!

For many of us, this is baffling. Why would they celebrate rules?

Well, to understand this, we must first understand how they viewed the law.

The word for "law" in Hebrew is *torah**. But there is, perhaps, a better translation of the word *torah*, one more in tune with the way Jewish people viewed these commands: instruction.

The Israelite people didn't see the *torah* as merely a set of rules and commands meant to demand obedience and catch people in our disobedience. They saw it as a gift of instruction.

They didn't view the *torah* as a form of oppression; they gave thanks for it. *Torah* showed them who they were. It set them apart as a people. It shaped their relationship with God.

Torah outlined how they were to live, which made them unique from everyone else on earth. It drew them closer to God, ordered them as a people, and supported their mission to be a blessing and reflect God's presence throughout the earth.

This is why Jesus said,

"DO NOT THINK THAT I HAVE COME TO ABOLISH THE LAW OR THE PROPHETS; I HAVE NOT COME TO ABOLISH THEM BUT TO FULFILL THEM"

MATTHEW 5:17

In other words, contrary to what I was often told growing up, Jesus didn't reject the *torah*. In fact, Jesus followed the *torah*. Never once did he break a command.

Jesus, like all Jewish people, saw the *torah* as a gift. And this should impact the way we see the *torah*.

The book of Acts shows how Gentile Christians were not required to follow all of the *torah* in order to be followers of Jesus. But this doesn't mean we should ignore the *torah*, as if it were outdated and obsolete.

As followers of Jesus, we should study it. We should wrestle with it. We should pray and discern which commands God still wants us to follow.

For, if the *torah* truly is a gift, then it would be foolish to ignore it.

How much time do you spend studying the Torah and other Old Testament scriptures?
How can you make this a more consistent part of your Bible study?

_____
_____
_____
_____
_____
_____

Read through the gospels and notice how many times Jesus quotes the Torah. What do these passages teach us?

_____
_____
_____
_____
_____
_____

What commands of scripture have you resisted? How might these actually be intended to be a blessing in your life?

_____
_____
_____
_____
_____
_____

RELATED SCRIPTURES TO STUDY

EXODUS 24:12   PSALM 1:2   PROVERBS 7:2

*Torah (capital T) refers to the Five Books of Moses. Lower case torah
refers to the general body of Jewish laws.

SANE & MISEO

SAW-NAY' & MIS-EH'-O

μισέω | שׂנא

> "If anyone comes to me and does not *hate* father and mother, wife and children, brothers and sisters—yes, even their own life—such a person cannot be my disciple."

Luke 14:26

Did you ever tell your parents, "I hate you!"

Television and movies make it feel as if this is some sort of right of passage that every child must go through.

You can just imagine the scene.

A teenager is told that he can't have the car for the night…

Or her parents say that she can't date the boy of her dreams…

Or a kid makes a giant plate of nachos, saving the most delicious chip for last, the one perfectly topped with every single element…and then dad eats it!

In each case, the result is the same. Someone screams "I hate you!"

It's such a powerful phrase. There is so much emotion wrapped up in three small words.

So, you can probably imagine the surprise of many people when they open up the Bible and find this passage, the one where Jesus says,

> "IF ANYONE COMES TO ME AND DOES NOT HATE FATHER AND MOTHER, WIFE AND CHILDREN, BROTHERS AND SISTERS—YES, EVEN THEIR OWN LIFE—SUCH A PERSON CANNOT BE MY DISCIPLE"
>
> LUKE 14:26

Hate!

Jesus just said that we have to hate our parents, our wife and kids, our siblings, and even ourselves in order to follow him.
Really?

Is Jesus really giving us permission to hate people? Is he commanding us to hate?

Something must be wrong with the translation.

Perhaps Luke somehow misquoted Jesus. Or maybe a monk was having a really bad day when copying the biblical manuscripts. Perhaps his sister was always more popular than him, his mom always forced him to eat his vegetables, and he was going through some pretty strong feelings about family while copying this portion of Luke's gospel.

It's possible, right?

Ok. Maybe not. But neither does the idea of Jesus telling us to hate those closest to us. It doesn't make sense that Jesus, whose whole message seems to be a message of love, would want us to hate anyone.

And the truth is: it shouldn't.

You see, all of this really comes down to how we understand words like "love" and "hate." In English, words like love and hate are words of emotion. They describe how we feel toward someone.

But that's not how they were understood by Jesus and his culture. When Jesus makes this statement about hating your family, Luke records the Greek word *miseo*. The Hebrew equivalent would be the word *sane*.

Sane doesn't mean "hate" as in an emotional feeling of hatred. That's because, in Hebrew, words like love and hate aren't words of emotion; they're words of action. They describe what you do.

To love something is to choose that thing. To hate it is to not choose it.

So, with this in mind, let's look at Luke 14:26 again. In this verse, Jesus isn't telling us that we need to feel the emotion of hate for our family members. He's saying that we have to choose Him!

If we want to be disciples of Jesus, we have to choose him over everything else in our lives – even our family. We have to surrender ourselves to him completely, follow him wherever he leads us, do whatever he calls us to do – even if that means choosing him over those we love most.

So, the next time you say "I love God" or "I hate this" – think about what you're really saying.

How true are those statements in your life?
Do you truly hate sin?
Do you truly hate poverty and evil and injustice?
And if so, what are you doing to actively choose something else?

Do you love God?
Do you choose God over everything else?
Even over the things you might say you love most?
Because in the end, Jesus isn't just inviting us into a relationship of feelings. He's inviting us into a relationship of action. And each day, we have a choice as to how we're going to act upon that relationship.

What are some things you need to hate (not choose) in your life so that you can love (choose) Jesus instead?

_____
_____
_____
_____
_____

What are some actions that you can take to better "hate" sin and "love" Jesus?

_____
_____
_____
_____
_____

How could your calendar better reflect the things that you "love" and "hate?"

_____
_____
_____
_____
_____

RELATED SCRIPTURES TO STUDY

EXODUS 20:5   MATTHEW 6:24

BEN

BANE

בֶּן

"The book of the generation of Jesus Christ, the *son* of David, the son of Abraham."

Matthew 1:1

ENGLISH TRANSLATION
SON

Have you ever read the beginning of Matthew's gospel? The part where he lists the lineage of Jesus?

I'll be honest, for most of my life, I skipped this. It just appeared to be 16 verses of names I couldn't pronounce.

I never could figure out why Matthew would choose to open his gospel this way. Aren't the opening lines supposed to be the hook for the entire story you're about to tell? This didn't seem like the ideal way to grab your reader's attention.

But that was because I wasn't a Jewish reader.

If I were a Jewish reader living at the time of Jesus, this opening statement by Matthew would have been incredibly captivating. You see, in the first century, genealogies mattered. A list of your ancestors was a powerful way to identify yourself to someone you just met.

Today, we introduce ourselves with our names, where we live, and our occupations. We believe these things define us and have value in our society.

But at the time of Jesus, it was your ancestors who identified you, who gave you value. There was an assumption at the time of Jesus that you were a reflection of your ancestors. It was assumed that you shared their same personality and values – for good or for bad.

If your father was honest, people assumed you were honest. At the same time, if your father was sinful, that stain could mark you as well.

And this didn't just apply to your parents. The word *ben*, which is the word for "son," could be used to refer not just to your child, but also to someone who was born generations later. Your lineage would either explain the greatness from which you descended, or the shame from which you were running,

…which is what makes Jesus' lineage SO interesting!

Just look at the people Matthew includes in Jesus' lineage, especially the women. Think about what he is trying to communicate through these names. What does this say about who Jesus is and what he represents?

Take, for example, Jesus' ancestor Jeconiah. Jeconiah is actually another name for King Jehoiachin. Jehoiachin was not a good king. He was the king of Judah when they were conquered by Babylon and sent into exile. He inaugurated one of the worst periods in Israelite history.

So why is he in Jesus' lineage?

Well, at the time of Jesus, people still felt the consequences of Jehoiachin's mistakes. The effects of the exile to Babylon still lingered. People were still oppressed. Their land was still not their own. It was out of the exile that many of the Messianic prophecies arose, prophecies that people were desperately clinging to at the time of Jesus.

But in connecting Jesus to Jehoiachin, Matthew isn't comparing Jesus to his ancestor; he contrasting him. He's saying to his audience: Jesus is a new kind of king! Whereas Jehoiachin caused the people to end up in exile and captivity, Jesus would be a King who would truly free them...and us.

Through this one word, *ben*, we learn not only about Jesus, but the people from whom he descends. He comes from a line of imperfect people, and he will be a savior for imperfect people.

This is the Good News! It gives us hope that no matter from whom we descend, no matter how bleak our past might be, our hope is in the one who can overcome any obstacle, the true Son of God: Jesus.

What aspects of your life do you believe truly define you? How might you introduce yourself to someone else, including those details you think matter most?	In what ways do you feel defined by your family and those who came before you?	What do the word *ben* and the names included in Jesus' lineage tell you about how God can overcome your past?

RELATED SCRIPTURES TO STUDY

GENESIS 10   **NUMBERS 1:1-16**   **LUKE 3:21-38**

MAKARIOS

MAK-AR'-EE-OS
μακάριος

"Blessed are the poor in spirit, for theirs is the kingdom of heaven."

Matthew 5:3

ENGLISH TRANSLATION
BLESSED

15 | MAKARIOS

Growing up, especially in church, I frequently heard people use the phrase "bless their heart."

This is a hilarious phrase. With it, you can say anything you want about someone, and still not appear offensive. It's as if the phrase "bless their heart" negates any intended insult.

For instance....

"That baby is the ugliest child I have ever seen.....bless his little heart."

Or....

"She is the meanest woman I have ever met in my life.....bless her heart."

Or....

"He's so creepy, he'd make a spider's skin crawl....
....Oh, I forgot....bless his heart!"

Do you see what I mean? It's as if it is a free pass to say anything you want.

But have you ever thought about what the phrase implies? Especially the word "bless." It is as if we are asking for some sort of reward or good fortune to be imparted upon the subject of our criticism.

That's what "bless" means, doesn't it? To receive some sort of reward or good fortune?

Here's the problem, though: this understanding of this one word actually causes us to misinterpret one of Jesus' most important teachings.

In his Sermon on the Mount, Jesus says phrases like "blessed are the poor in spirit," "blessed are the meek," and "blessed are the peacemakers." We interpret these verses to mean that when someone is, for example, poor in spirit, that person will be rewarded or experience good fortune.

But that is not what Jesus means.

The word that is translated "blessed" is actually the Greek word *makarios*. There is no good translation for *makarios* in English. In many ways, this is because of how we put our English sentences together.

You see, in English, every sentence needs a subject. Even sentences that don't explicitly include a subject still imply a subject. So when Jesus says, "Blessed are the poor in spirit," our immediate question – whether we realize it or not – is "WHO is doing the blessing?" And our natural assumption, of course, is God. The poor in spirit are blessed because God blessed them.*

But when we do that, we turn *makarios* into a transactional sort of word. God is blessing us because of what we do or the situation we are in. God is the blesser and we are the blessed.

But that's not what *makarios* is suggesting. A better translation for *makarios* is "You will feel truly content when…" So, if we were to re-translate Jesus' statements in Matthew 5, we might say something like…

"You will feel truly content when you are poor in spirit, for yours is the kingdom of heaven."

Or…"You will feel truly content when you are a peacemaker, for you will be called a child of God."

In other words, you can feel truly content, even when you're poor because you are experiencing the Kingdom of Heaven. You can feel truly content when you're a peacemaker because you're experiencing what it means to be a child of God.

It is not that God is rewarding us for being in these positions. It is that we are accepting the invitation to experience something available to us, even in those positions. We are embracing *makarios*.

How has this insight about *makarios* changed the way you read the Beatitudes?	In what areas of your life do you feel like you are experiencing *makarios*? Where in your life do you feel truly blessed, truly surrendered to Jesus?	In what ways might you still be trying to save yourself and instead need to trust Jesus alone to be your Savior?
_____		_____
_____	_____	_____
_____	_____	_____
_____	_____	_____
_____	_____	_____
_____	_____	_____
_____	_____	

RELATED SCRIPTURES TO STUDY

LUKE 14:12-15   **JAMES 1:12**   **REVELATION 14:13**

For a more in-depth explanation of makarios, refer to "Misreading Scripture with Western Eyes: Removing Cultural Blinders to Better Understand the Bible" by E. Randolph Richards & Brandon J. O'Brien, 2012.

MAGOI

MAG'-OI
μάγοι

"After Jesus was born in Bethlehem in Judea, during the time of King Herod, *Magi* from the east came to Jerusalem."

Matthew 2:2

Have you ever realized that something you believed about the Bible wasn't actually true? I've had a few of these moments throughout my life,

...like when I realized that the Bible never says that Adam and Eve ate an "apple"
...or that it never says that Jonah was swallowed by a "whale"
...or that the gospels say that Jesus used five loaves and two fish to feed 5,000 men PLUS women and children.

Sometimes these insights are simply a matter of replacing one detail with another. But there are also instances in which the differences between what we believe and what scripture actually says can significantly impact the meaning of a passage.

Take, for instance, the story of the three "kings" in Matthew 2. Every year in December, homes are adorned with nativities complete with three kingly figures. Churches join together in the chorus of "We Three Kings."

But the Bible never says there were THREE kings present at the birth of Christ. In fact, scripture never even says they were KINGS. And this makes a big difference in how we understand this story.

The word that we translate "kings" is actually the Greek word *magoi*. This is the root of our English word "magician." Magi weren't kings. If anything, they were people who worked for kings. Magi were similar to astronomers or astrologers. They would study the stars and attempt to predict future events.

Outside of the Bible, in Greek literature, the term magi is used to describe people from places like Babylon or Parthia (what is now modern-day Iran and Iraq). This is reflected in the gifts they bring to Jesus. Gold was mined in Arabia. Frankincense and myrrh were harvested from trees that only grew in this region.

These details tell us something significant about magi: they were Gentiles.

While this may not matter much to us today, it was crucial (and surprising) to those listening to this gospel 2,000 years ago.

At the time in which Matthew is writing this gospel, many new Christians were not of Jewish descent. They were converts to the Jewish Messiah. And in the early church, there was much tension between Jews and Gentiles – even between Jewish and Gentile Christians. Paul's letter to the Romans focuses, in great part, on addressing the tension between these groups and the belief by some that Gentile Christians were inferior to Jewish Christians.

So by sharing this story, Matthew, a Jewish disciple of Jesus, is making a profound statement: Jesus came for both! Jesus came for ALL!

Then, as now, there has always been the temptation to divide ourselves....

Worthy vs. unworthy
Superior vs. inferior
Important vs. less important

But with this one word, *magoi*, Matthew reminds us that those who were considered unworthy, inferior, less important were among the first to meet the Savior of the world.

Are there people in your life who try to make you think that you aren't good enough? Or that you aren't worthy of God's love?	Are there reasons you don't think you're worthy of the salvation that Jesus offers?	Who are the people around you who are told they "aren't good enough"? How might you share the Good News of the gospel with them?
_____	_____	_____
_____	_____	_____
_____	_____	_____
_____	_____	_____
_____	_____	_____
_____	_____	_____
_____	_____	_____
_____	_____	_____
_____	_____	_____
_____	_____	_____
_____	_____	_____
_____	_____	_____
_____	_____	_____

RELATED SCRIPTURES TO STUDY

ACTS 13:5-8

YIRAH

YIR-AW'

יראה

"And he will delight in the
fear of the Lord."

Isaiah 11:3

FEAR

When I was very litttle, I went to a friend's house around Halloween. While I was there, his older brothers decided it would be fun to scare us. They owned terrifying rubber masks that depicted a maniacal clown and a hideous ghoul. While we were playing, they would walk into the room or jump out from behind a door wearing these masks.

It was terrifying!

At the time, I didn't realize what was happening. I truly believed that these creatures were in the house. So I would navigate the hallways in fear and trepidation. I would ask my friend's parents to accompany me everywhere I went. I had nightmares for weeks.

This is one of the first things I think of when I hear the word fear. I think of monstrous figures who desire to harm you. I think of the timidity and vulnerability I felt as a child.

Perhaps you have similar things that filled you with fear as a child.
Some of those things still might fill you with fear.

But here's the thing: I have never felt this way about God.

I was always confused by verses in the Bible that talked about fearing God. Never did I associate God with the images and feelings that came to mind when I thought of those Halloween masks.

In fact, I have always had the opposite belief about God. God is the one who frees us from fear.

So why does scripture tell us to fear God?

And how are we to understand passages that say things like,

"AND HE WILL DELIGHT IN THE FEAR OF THE LORD"

ISAIAH 11:3

Are we really supposed to be afraid of God? Why would we delight in this?

Fear in our culture often assumes the threat of harm: the thing that we fear either could harm or has harmed us.

But this is not necessarily how the Israelite people understood fear – at least not when it came to their relationship with God.

The Hebrew word for "fear" is *yirah*. The Greek equivalent is *phobos*. It is a word that suggests a deep reverence, a sense of awe, a state in which we are overwhelmed with wonder. In fact, many times, what is translated "reverence" in our English translations is actually *yirah*, the word for "fear."

Our fear of the Lord is a consequence of how we see God, and how we see ourselves. To fear the Lord requires that we humble ourselves so that we might realize how small we are compared to how great God is.

We have a relationship with the God of the universe, the one who created the sun, the moon, and the stars; the God who sees all, knows all, and has the power to control all.

This God is the one who has given us life, who holds the keys to our salvation, and who, out of love for us, has given us free will.

To fear God is to be in awe of such power and love, to be grateful for what God has done and who God has created us to be. To fear God is to realize that God owes us nothing and yet chooses to give us everything we hold dear in our lives. And to fear God is to respond to such realizations with wonder and worship.

When we fear God, we obey God, we serve God, and we surrender our lives to God.

We do these things not because we are scared of God's reprisal but because we know that God and God alone is worthy of such devotion.

God's glory and power compel us to fear. And our fear, in turn, compels us to worship.

How does knowing the meaning of *yirah* change the way you understand what it means to "fear" God?	What are some ways you can take time to truly appreciate just how awesome, wonderful, and powerful God is?	What are some ways you can help others to see how awesome, wonderful, and powerful God is?

RELATED SCRIPTURES TO STUDY

GENESIS 20:11   **PSALM 34:11**   **EPHESIANS 5:21**

YESHUA

YAY-SHOO-AH'

ישוע

"And she will bring forth a Son, and you shall call His name *Jesus*, for He will save His people from their sins."

Matthew 1:21

ENGLISH TRANSLATION
GOD SAVES

Do you know what your name means?

I remember having a bookmark when I was a child that had my name on it. Below my name, it had the image of a mountain and said: "from a beacon on a hill." Apparently, this is what my name means.

The name Brandon has either Celtic or Anglo-Saxon roots and has been in use for hundreds of years. It even derives from the Irish word for a prince or king.

But none of this was on my parents' minds when they gave me this name. In fact, I think I was supposed to be named "Brandy," given the fact that, when I was born, my nursery had already been painted pink and all of my clothes were dresses.

The truth is, we don't put much emphasis on the meaning of names in western culture. And believe it or not, this impacts how we read the Bible.

We read names like Adam, Moses, and Ruth, and we simply see them as names, appellations we use to refer to the characters in the Bible. But these names have meanings, which are actually quite important when understanding the scriptures in which their stories are told.

This is also true with Jesus. In fact, this is especially true when it comes to Jesus.

When the angel comes to Joseph in Matthew's gospel, the angel says of Mary,

> "AND SHE WILL BRING FORTH A SON, AND YOU SHALL CALL HIS NAME JESUS, FOR HE WILL SAVE HIS PEOPLE FROM THEIR SINS"
>
> MATTHEW 1:21

The word for "Jesus" in Greek is *iēsous*. But *iēsous* is actually the Greek version of the Hebrew word *Yeshua* or *Yehoshua*.

This is how people would have referred to Jesus. They would have called him *Yeshua* ben Yoseph: *Yeshua*, the son of Joseph.

Yeshua is actually the word for the Hebrew name Joshua, which was an incredibly common Jewish name in the first-century community in which Jesus lived. But even though this name was common, it was a name that had significant meaning!

Yeshua means God helps; God saves; God delivers. This explains why, immediately after commanding that they name him Jesus, the angel says he will save his people from their sins. Jesus' very name promises salvation.

To people living under the oppressive rule of the Roman empire in the first century, his name promised that God would save them.

To people like you and me living today, Jesus' name promises deliverance in the face of other trials and tribulations.

This gives a whole new meaning to the idea of calling upon the name of Jesus. Every time we speak his name and pray for his help, we are proclaiming our belief in a God who saves.

This is the good news of the gospel. Jesus' very name proclaims it. We are not left alone to struggle in this world. We are not left to carry our own burdens and fight our own battles.

We have a Savior. His name is Jesus. And that very name is a promise in which we can put our complete trust.

How have you experienced salvation through Jesus in your life?	Who in your life needs to hear the good news about God who saves?	Where in your life do you need to trust that Jesus will save you?

RELATED SCRIPTURES TO STUDY

ZECHARIAH 3

DAY 19

MASHIACH & CHRISTOS

MAW-SHEE'-AKH & KHRIS-TOS'

משיח | Χριστός

ENGLISH TRANSLATION
ANOINTED ONE

19 | MASHIACH & CHRISTOS

Have you ever wondered what Jesus' full name was?

In the very first verse of Mark's gospel, Mark refers to Jesus as *iēsous christos*, which we translate as Jesus Christ.

Does this mean that Jesus was his first name, and Christ was his last name?

Was his mother Mary Christ?
His father Joseph Christ?
His siblings James, Joey, and Tammy Christ?
Did they have a labradoodle named Buddy Christ (BC for short)? But when Jesus was born, they changed his name to Another Dog because, obviously, everything shifted from BC to AD?

By now, you probably realize that the answer to all of these questions is simply: no. When Mark refers to Jesus as iēsous *christos*, *christos* isn't Jesus' last name. It's his title.

Christos, which is actually a Greek translation of the Hebrew word *mashiach*, means "anointed one." This is where we get the word Messiah. By using this term, Mark is making sure that, from the very outset of his gospel, we know that Jesus is the Savior for whom we've been waiting.

With this one word, Mark is setting the tone for this whole story he's about to tell! He wants us to know that whoever we are, whatever we're going through as we read these words, whatever troubles we find ourselves in, we have hope.

Our Messiah has come. The world is different now. And we don't have to be afraid because salvation is here!

We don't have to worry if Jesus is just some great prophet or if his presence really makes a difference in this world. His very name tells us who he is.

He is our Savior.
He is our *mashiach*.
He is the Christ!

Read some of the additional scriptures below. How does the meaning of the word *christos* impact how you understand these passages?

_____
_____
_____
_____
_____

In what ways are you relying upon Jesus to be your *christos*, your Messiah right now?

_____
_____
_____
_____
_____

Are there things or people other than Jesus that you're tempted to look to for salvation? Things like money? Power? Success? Political leaders?

_____
_____
_____
_____
_____

RELATED SCRIPTURES TO STUDY

DANIEL 9:25-26   MATTHEW 24:5,23   ACTS 18:28

DAY 20

SHAYM

SHAME

שם

"Thou shalt not take the *name* of the LORD thy God in vain."

Exodus 20:7

The first church I ever pastored on my own was a small church in a small town. We lived in a house just down the street from the church on the main road in town. Even though it was the main road, it wasn't very busy. For example, one evening, a friend of mine commented on how heavy traffic was getting in town. And when I looked down the street, all I saw were two dogs and a tractor.

Nevertheless, even though the road wasn't heavily trafficked, it was policed. A local police officer would park in front of our church in order to catch those exceeding the 35-mile-per-hour speed limit.

…And one day, he caught my wife.

As she pulled into our driveway, he pulled up behind her. She stepped out of the car thinking he was welcoming us to town. "Hi, I'm LeeAnn," she said as she walked back to his car. He returned her greeting with a flat "License and registration."

We were new to town, and she wasn't used to the speed limit, so he let her off with a warning. But I'm sure you can imagine how humiliating that was for her: the preacher's wife gets pulled over in front of the church on her first week in town.

Police officers have a saying when they want someone to pull over – at least they do in the movies. They shout, "Stop in the name of the law!"

Have you ever heard that phrase?
Have you ever wondered what it means?
What exactly is the "name" of the law?

Well, understanding this phrase can actually help us to understand the true meaning of many different scriptures.

When the police tell someone to stop in the name of the law, they aren't claiming that the word "law" has any power. What they mean is that they are invoking the authority of the law. They bear its name. They represent the law.

This same understanding is present throughout scripture. The Hebrew word for "name" is *shaym*. But *shaym* refers to more than just the word you use to address someone. *Shaym* refers to a person's identity, their authority. To bear a person's name means that you are that person's representative.

This changes the way we understand many familiar scriptures. For instance, when God says,

"THOU SHALT NOT TAKE THE NAME OF THE LORD THY GOD IN VAIN"

EXODUS 20:7

God isn't talking about using God's name as part of a curse word. God is talking about how we represent God in this world.

This is also the case when Jesus says,

"NO ONE WHO PERFORMS A MIRACLE IN MY NAME WILL SOON BE ABLE TO SPEAK EVIL OF ME"

MARK 9:39

Jesus isn't referring to people who simply say the word "Jesus." Jesus' name isn't a magical phrase. His name represents his identity, his authority. Those who do things in Jesus' name are representing him.

In the end, this isn't a matter of simply saying the right words. It's deeper than that. It speaks to our relationship with Jesus, how we represent him in the world.

Do we truly bear his name well?
Or do we take his name in vain?

Read the additional scriptures listed below. How does this understanding of the word *shaym* change the way you interpret these passages?	What are some ways that you intentionally bear Jesus' name in this world?	What do you think it means for us to take Jesus' name in vain?

RELATED SCRIPTURES TO STUDY

ISAIAH 25:1   **MICAH 6:9**   **JOHN 14:14**

SHALOM

SHAW-LOME'

שלום

"But the Lord said to him, '*Peace!* Do not be afraid. You are not going to die.' So Gideon built an altar to the Lord there and called it The Lord Is *Peace*."

Judges 6:23-24

When I was in Middle School, Peace Frog shirts were really popular. Do you remember those? What a strange trend.

Every generation has trends that don't make any sense in retrospect: mullets, Pet Rocks, the Thigh Master. My generation can claim Peace Frogs.

What was the point of the peace frog? Were we really promoting peace? Did we believe that we could change the world one amphibian-covered t-shirt at a time?

If so, we weren't the first. It seems that generations have been longing for peace since the beginning of time. In fact, peace is a substantial theme within the Old Testament. The Hebrew word for peace, *shalom*, appears over 150 times.

For instance, in Judges 6, the Israelite people are being oppressed by the Midianites. Once again, an outside nation has come into Israel and has taken control. But the Midianites haven't just taken control of Israelite lands; they've kicked the Israelite people out.

The Israelites are hiding in caves. They hardly have any place to grow food. They're suffering.

And in the midst of this, God comes to a man named Gideon. The angel of God promises that God is with them. But here's the crazy thing: Gideon doesn't believe him.

Gideon says:

> "EXCUSE ME, MY LORD. IF YAHWEH IS WITH US, WHY THEN HAS ALL THIS HAPPENED TO US? WHERE ARE ALL HIS WONDERFUL DEEDS THAT OUR ANCESTORS RECOUNTED TO US, SAYING, 'DID NOT YAHWEH BRING

US UP FROM EGYPT?' BUT NOW YAHWEH HAS FORSAKEN US; HE HAS GIVEN US INTO THE PALM OF MIDIAN"

JUDGES 6:13

Have you ever felt like that?

And when God tells Gideon that God will use him to free the people, Gideon responds by pointing out that he isn't good enough. His clan is weakest. He's the youngest in his family. God has picked the wrong person.

In other words, Gideon is filled with doubt.

He doubts that God is with them.
He doubts that God can use him.
And he doubts that God is even speaking to him right now.

But then something clicks; Gideon realizes that all of this is true. And it's in response to this revelation that Gideon builds an altar and calls it "The Lord is *Shalom*" – The Lord is peace.

But what is so easy to miss is the depth of these words. *Shalom* isn't just talking about what God has done. *Shalom* is also a word that highlights what God will do: that this is the God who will bring peace to Israel.

But there's more!

Even the word peace means more than we tend to think it does. *Shalom* doesn't just mean the absence of war. *Shalom* also communicates this idea of wholeness or completeness.

What this means is that God isn't just going to remove the Midianites and end the fighting. Gideon has faith that the Israelite people will be whole again. They're in this current situation because their hearts turned away from God. But now, their relationship with God will be whole.

This is true peace. True *shalom* comes when our relationships are made whole again, then the broken parts of our lives and our world become complete.

Shalom is the good news of the gospel: that God will no longer allow this world to remain broken. But God has sent to us the Prince of Peace – the Prince of *Shalom* – who will restore our relationship with God and transform us into the complete picture of who God originally created us to be.

How does your new understanding of the word *shalom* impact your understanding of
what it means for the Lord to be our peace?

_____
_____
_____
_____
_____
_____
_____
_____
_____
_____

What are ways that you can share *shalom* with others?

_____
_____
_____
_____
_____
_____
_____
_____
_____
_____
_____

RELATED SCRIPTURES TO STUDY

GENESIS 28:20-22   PSALM 72:3   ISAIAH 38:17

AION

AHEE-OHN'
αἰών

"Anyone who speaks a word against the Son of Man will be forgiven, but anyone who speaks against the Holy Spirit will not be forgiven, either in this *age* or in the age to come."

Matthew 12:32

There was always a verse in the Bible that worried me as a child. I became so nervous the first time I read Jesus' words in Matthew when he says,

"ANYONE WHO SPEAKS AGAINST THE HOLY SPIRIT WILL NOT BE FORGIVEN, EITHER IN THIS AGE OR IN THE AGE TO COME"

MATTHEW 12:32B

I understood this to mean that there was at least one sin that was unforgivable. I wasn't sure exactly what it meant to speak against the Holy Spirit. But I didn't want to do it. I didn't even want to accidentally do it. The consequences seemed too great.

As far as I could tell, Jesus was saying that if I did this, I wouldn't be forgiven and I wouldn't be allowed into heaven.

The phrase that I was interpreting to mean heaven was "the age to come." I assumed that since we now live on earth, and in the future we will live in heaven, the age to come must be a reference to heaven.

Have you ever interpreted this verse that way?

But in making this assumption, I was missing something significant about how Jesus and the Jewish people thought in the first century.

You see, today, in western culture, we view time as linear. There was a beginning. There is a present. And there will be an end. At any given moment, we fall somewhere along this timeline.

But that is not how Jesus is expressing time in this verse from Matthew's gospel.

The word that we translate "age" is the Greek word *aion*. An age is a period of time that has a beginning and an end. There is no specified length of time that an age must last. It is simply that when one age ends, a new age will begin.

At the time of Jesus, this term also had Messianic undertones. *Aion* could also be a reference to a Messianic period – present or future.

These nuances impact how we interpret Jesus' words in the Matthew 12 passage. When Jesus referenced the present age and the age to come, he was describing the age that people currently lived in and a new age that would come.

While Jesus does tell us throughout the gospels about a heaven where we abide with God beyond the bonds of earth, there was also a dominant belief within the Jewish community that the "age to come" was going to come here on earth. Creation would be restored and God would reign on earth.

So, when Jesus talks about the consequences of speaking against the Holy Spirit, he has this in mind as well. He is saying that such an act will impact us both in the current state of things and when those things change. Our relationship with God will be affected both now and when God restores this world; in this age, and in the age to come.

Read the additional scriptures below. How does this understanding of *aion* impact how you interpret these scriptures?	What are some challenges you're facing in this current age?	What hope do these scriptures give you for the "age to come"?

RELATED SCRIPTURES TO STUDY

MATTHEW 13:49   1 TIMOTHY 6:19   TITUS 2:12

HAGAH

HAW-GAW'

הגה

"Keep this Book of the Law always on your lips; **meditate** on it day and night, so that you may be careful to do everything written in it. Then you will be prosperous and successful."

Joshua 1:8

ENGLISH TRANSLATION
MEDITATE

When I was in my first year of seminary, they required all of us to attend a weekend long retreat of complete silence.

The setting was beautiful. The retreat center was situated upon a hill overlooking majestic forests and beautiful gardens. And for thirty-six hours or so, we allowed ourselves to set aside the noise and distraction of our everyday lives, and simply rest in the presence of the Lord.

I read.
I slept.
I took long walks around the grounds.
I stressed out when I couldn't figure out how to turn on the shower and had no way to ask! (My poor roommate!)

In the end, it was the silence of the retreat that allowed me to hear God's voice more clearly over those few days.

This is what I think of when I think of a word like meditation: a period of silence where we quiet our minds so that we can hear God speak.

As far as I've always understood it, meditation is something that should be done in silence. You can be in a garden, or in a room filled with pillows, or sitting in your car outside a Dairy Queen. Regardless, meditation is silent.

But apparently, that is not necessarily how Jesus and the people of the Jewish community viewed it.

When we hear a verse like,

"KEEP THIS BOOK OF THE LAW ALWAYS ON YOUR LIPS; MEDITATE ON IT DAY AND NIGHT"
JOSHUA 1:8

we assume that scripture is commanding us to silently reflect upon God's Word. But the word we translate "meditate" (hagah) actually means something different.

Throughout the Old Testament scriptures, hagah can refer to a variety of sounds such as a lion's growl (Isaiah 31:4) or a dove's moan (Isaiah 38:14). What verses like these help us to see is that meditation isn't merely silent reflection; it's also verbalized reflection.

Meditation can be silent. But it can also take the form of dancing, singing, or simply vocalizing our prayers to God.

It is our opportunity to express to God what we are thinking, feeling, and learning as we reflect on God's Word and God's presence in our lives.

It is a reminder that our relationship with God is part of our nature. The growls and groans remind us that every part of creation was formed to worship and communicate with our Creator.

We are here to seek and desire the Lord. This is what God desires of us, whatever form it might take.

What are some ways you have meditated upon the Lord in the past?	How does this understanding of *hagah* free you to explore new practices?	How does this understanding of *hagah* impact the way you imagine moments like Jesus going to pray on the mountainside?

RELATED SCRIPTURES TO STUDY

ISAIAH 31:4   **ISAIAH 38:14**   **ISAIAH 59:11**

AYIN TOVAH & AYIN RA'AH

AH'-YIN TO-VAW' & AH'-YIN RAW-AW'

עין רעת | עין טובה

"The eye is the lamp of the body. If your *eyes* are *healthy*, your whole body will be full of light. But if your *eyes* are *unhealthy*, your whole body will be full of darkness. If then the light within you is darkness, how great is that darkness!"

Matthew 6:22-23

ENGLISH TRANSLATION
GOOD EYE/BAD EYE

24 | AYIN TOVAH & AYIN RA'AH

There is something about a new year that inspires me.

In December, I'll put off cleaning, binge on Christmas cookies, skip my workouts, and let my hair grow long (and by "long," I mean about half an inch because, you know, alopecia).

But as soon as the calendar turns to January 1st, everything changes.

I start a new exercise routine.
I am strict about my eating.
I summon my inner Marie Kondo and organize all of my socks in alphabetical order.

There is just something about the transition to a new year that gives me an eye for the future.

That's an interesting phrase, isn't it? An "eye" for the future.

As soon as you read it, you understood what it meant. It indicates the way in which someone sees the world.

Well, did you know that people used similar language at the time of Jesus?

In scripture, there are regular references to our "eyes." The only problem is, we rarely see them.

Let me give you some examples…

In Proverbs, we read:

> **"THE GENEROUS WILL THEMSELVES BE BLESSED, FOR THEY SHARE THEIR FOOD WITH THE POOR"**
> **PROVERBS 22:9**

Later, we read:

> **"THE STINGY ARE EAGER TO GET RICH AND ARE UNAWARE THAT POVERTY AWAITS THEM"**
> **PROVERBS 28:22**

Now, in neither of these verses do we see the word "eye" – at least not in English. But it is very apparent in the Hebrew.

The phrase translated "generous" is the Hebrew phrase *ayin tovah*. It literally means "good eye."

Similarly, the phrase translated "stingy" is *ayin ra'ah*. It literally means "bad eye."

These were common idioms in Hebrew culture. And they give us insight into the teachings of Jesus.

At one point, Jesus says,

> ## "THE EYE IS THE LAMP OF THE BODY. IF YOUR EYES ARE HEALTHY, YOUR WHOLE BODY WILL BE FULL OF LIGHT. BUT IF YOUR EYES ARE UNHEALTHY, YOUR WHOLE BODY WILL BE FULL OF DARKNESS. IF THEN THE LIGHT WITHIN YOU IS DARKNESS, HOW GREAT IS THAT DARKNESS!"
> ### MATTHEW 6:22-23

If you're like me, you might have interpreted this passage to mean that we must look kindly upon people; we must not lust; we must be careful about what we look at and how we interpret things.

But that isn't really the point Jesus is making. Jesus is making this statement in the midst of a teaching about storing up treasures in heaven, right after he has just said,

> # "WHERE YOUR TREASURE IS, YOUR HEART WILL BE ALSO"
> ## MATTHEW 6:21

Ultimately, what Jesus is saying is that if you have good eyes, if you are generous, then your whole body will be filled with light. And if you have bad eyes, if you are greedy, then your whole life will be filled with darkness,
...which brings me back to the subject of a new year.

When a new year begins, we often have our eyes upon the future. But our focus, more often than not, tends to be very personal, very self-focused. We make plans for how we will improve our appearance, or improve our health, or achieve our goals.

Our eyes are focused inward.

But what if we chose to begin the year with "good eyes," instead; with *ayin tovah*?

What if we decided to begin the year focusing outward? What if we decided that the most important goal before us wasn't just self-improvement, but Kingdom advancement?

What if we set goals for how we were going to bless others, share the gospel, and further Christ's work in this world?

These are the kinds of eyes God wants us to have. This is *ayin tovah*.

What would it look like for you to begin to see the world with *ayin tovah* [good eyes]?

_____

_____

_____

_____

_____

_____

_____

Perhaps you're reading this in the summer or fall. What is an event or date you can look to as a compelling "starting point" upon which to begin working at seeing the world with "good eyes"?

_____

_____

_____

_____

_____

_____

_____

_____

Who can you invite to help and hold you accountable as you try to see the world with this new perspective?

_____

_____

_____

_____

_____

_____

_____

_____

RELATED SCRIPTURES TO STUDY

DEUTERONOMY 15:9   PROVERBS 22:9

BARAK

BAW-RAK'

ברך

"I will *bless* the LORD at all times:
his praise shall continually be in
my mouth."

Psalm 34:1

ENGLISH TRANSLATION
BLESS

25 | BARAK

When I was an Associate Pastor, I served at a church that took an annual mission trip to South Florida. The ministry we supported down there was amazing. There are few places on earth where I have felt God's presence so palpably and abundantly.

But about a month after my first trip to this ministry, the entire facility burned to the ground. Someone in the community set fire to their buildings and almost everything was destroyed.

Nevertheless, the ministry continued. Within weeks, they had modified all of their activities and were already making plans to rebuild.

We had the opportunity to go down there again the following year. It was amazing. The faith and resilience we witnessed were overwhelming.

While we were there, we spent an evening in prayer. We broke into small groups and each person had the opportunity to request prayer for something specific. Some people prayed for the ministry. Others prayed for challenges in their own lives. But one girl prayed for something that completely surprised me.

She prayed for God.

I had never thought of doing such a thing. Why would we pray for God? Isn't God the one we pray to? Does it even make sense to pray for God?

As I was reading scripture, I discovered another situation that brought forth similar questions in my mind. Throughout the Psalms, I discovered the phrase "Bless the Lord."

For instance, in Psalm 34, we read:

"I WILL BLESS THE LORD AT ALL TIMES: HIS PRAISE SHALL CONTINUALLY BE IN MY MOUTH"

PSALM 34:1

That didn't make sense to me either. How can we bless the Lord? Isn't God the one who blesses us?

But as I began to investigate the true meaning of this phrase, I realized something. The Hebrew word for "bless" is *barak*. But *barak* is also related to another Hebrew word: *berek*. *Berek* is the word for "knee."

This is no accident.

The connection between these two words reminds us that when we come before the Lord, we are meant to come to our knees, to kneel in worship. To say that we "bless the Lord" means that we worship God both for who God is and what God has done.

This becomes apparent as we look at other Psalms that include variations of *barak*. For instance, Psalm 68 says,

"BLESSED BE THE LORD, WHO DAILY LOADETH US WITH BENEFITS, EVEN THE GOD OF OUR SALVATION"
PSALM 68:19

The blessing is an act of worship, a response of praise and adoration.

This changed the way that I saw the prayer of this child. I realized that she wasn't lifting up the Lord's name because she thought God needed help. She was doing it as an act of worship. She was focusing her heart, placing God before herself in this time of prayer, showing greater concern for God than her own needs.

It was a powerful act of worship. And it has forever changed the way that I approach God myself.

How has the meaning of *barak* changed the way you understand what it means to "bless" God?	What are some areas in your life where you need to bless God?	How does this change your understanding of a "blessing" before a meal? Should you be blessing the food, or blessing God?
_____	_____	_____
_____	_____	_____
_____	_____	_____
_____	_____	_____
_____	_____	_____
_____	_____	_____

RELATED SCRIPTURES TO STUDY

JOB 2:9   PSALM 103:2   PSALM 135:19

AMEN

AW-MANE'

אמן

"Blessed be the LORD God
of Israel for ever and ever.
And all the people said,
Amen, and praised the LORD."

1 Chronicles 16:36

ENGLISH TRANSLATION
I AGREE

How do you say the word *amen*?

Do you pronounce it "ah-men"? Or "ay-men"?
Do you get really excited and pronounce it "ay-may-an!"?
In the church I attended growing up, there was a man who always said, "*Amen....
and sometimes women!*"

But what does this word really mean? Is it just a made-up word created solely
to conclude prayers? Or does it have a deeper meaning?

Well, to begin, did you realize that *amen* is actually a Hebrew word? And it is related
to two other Hebrew words: *emet* and *emun*. *Emet* means truth. And *emun* means
faith or trust.

So to say *amen* is to communicate something along the lines of "I believe this to
be true" or "I affirm this."

That is quite different from what I assumed growing up. I always assumed that *amen*
meant something to the effect of "the end." It was a word we used to conclude every
prayer. We sang it at the end of every hymn.

But this is different. Used this way, the word *amen* is a commitment of agreement. It
affirms the prayer being spoken. It professes faith in the words being sung.

This explains why, in Jewish culture, the word *amen* wasn't said by the person offering
the prayer or singing the hymn. It was declared by the congregation. The congregation
was proclaiming that they agreed with the words that had been said, and they also
offered those words to God.

Amen is a word that connects us. It is a reminder that prayer isn't merely a solitary
practice between one person and God. Prayer connects us all. Prayer reminds us that
we share a common faith, a common mission, and a common heart. We are on this
journey together.

And to that, may we all say: *Amen.*

How have you typically understood *amen* in the past?

_____
_____
_____
_____
_____
_____
_____
_____

How might this understanding of *amen* impact the way you end your prayers?

_____
_____
_____
_____
_____
_____
_____
_____
_____

How does this understanding of *amen* impact the way you view the additional scriptures below?

_____
_____
_____
_____
_____
_____
_____
_____
_____

RELATED SCRIPTURES TO STUDY

DEUTERONOMY 27:15-26   ISAIAH 65:16   JEREMIAH 11:5

RAV

RAWV

רַב

"But the **commander** left behind some of the poorest people of the land to work the vineyards and fields."

2 Kings 25:12

I grew up in church. Within a few weeks of making my entrance into the world, I was making my way down the aisle to be baptized. Every week, my extended family would gather in our two pews (I say "our" pews because, while our names weren't on them, the cushions were perfectly molded to our personal posteriors). We would sing hymns, hear sermons, and praise God together.

As time passed, I became very familiar with the songs we sang in church. I would sing them throughout the week. Many of the lyrics are still imprinted upon my mind.

But I realized something recently. For most of my life, I really had no idea what those lyrics truly meant. I knew the name of Jesus and that he was our Savior. I knew about his miracles, his death on the cross, his resurrection on Easter.

But it wasn't until I was older that I understood the fullness of those truths and how intimately relevant they were to my life.

The more I study the original words of scripture, the more I have this same sort of experience: I discover a much deeper meaning to a familiar idea.

This was definitely the case when I learned the truth behind the word rabbi.

If you've been following these devotions in order, you probably remember that on Day 10, I also talked about rabbis. But the fact that there is more to discover about this one word actually highlights my point: there are incredible depths to be explored in even a single word.

Rabbi finds its roots in the Hebrew word *rav*. *Rav* is a word that literally means great, much, many, and sometimes even commander. Early on, it was used to refer to military leaders or other people in power. But as time progressed, *rav* transformed into words like rabbi or rabboni. Even at the time of Jesus, these words were primarily a reference to the master of a slave or disciple.

Let me say that again: both a slave and a disciple would refer to their master as rabbi.

This adds another level to our understanding of the relationship between Jesus and his disciples. They didn't just follow Jesus. He wasn't just their teacher. They were devoted to him like a slave is to his master.

I, personally, don't enjoy this imagery. A word like "slave" evokes images of pain, suffering, and injustice.

But the extreme nature of this imagery serves a purpose. When Jesus invites us to be his disciples, it is essential for us to understand the level of devotion he expects of us. Disciples didn't hesitate to go wherever their rabbis wanted them to go. They would immediately follow any instruction their rabbi gave them.

In fact, it was said that

"ALL ACTS A SLAVE PERFORMS FOR HIS MASTER, A DISCIPLE PERFORMS FOR HIS RABBI"

KETUBOT 96A*

For many of us, this changes what it looks like to be a disciple of Jesus. To be a disciple is to fully surrender our lives to Christ.

No amount of time is too much. No task is too great. Our lives are entirely devoted to him.

As Paul says in his letter to the Romans:

"DO YOU NOT KNOW THAT IF YOU PRESENT YOURSELVES TO ANYONE AS OBEDIENT SLAVES, YOU ARE SLAVES OF THE ONE WHOM YOU OBEY, EITHER OF SIN, WHICH LEADS TO DEATH, OR OF OBEDIENCE, WHICH LEADS TO RIGHTEOUSNESS?"

ROMANS 6:16

And given the choice between sin and our Savior, we gladly choose Christ.

How does the definition of *rav* impact the way you understand what it means to be a disciple of Jesus?

_____
_____
_____
_____
_____
_____
_____

Can we truly call ourselves "disciples" of Jesus if we only follow him when it is comfortable and convenient?

_____
_____
_____
_____
_____
_____
_____
_____
_____

What in your life do you need to surrender to Jesus in order for him to truly be your rabbi?

_____
_____
_____
_____
_____
_____
_____
_____

RELATED SCRIPTURES TO STUDY

GENESIS 25:23   PROVERBS 28:16   JEREMIAH 39:13

*Ketubot is a tractate found in the Jewish Talmud, a text comprised of
the Mishnah (Jewish oral tradition) and Gemara (an elucidation on the Mishnah).

ASAR & HITIR

AW-SAR' & HEE-TEER

התר | אסר

"I will give you the keys of the kingdom of heaven; whatever you *bind* on earth will be bound in heaven, and whatever you *loose* on earth will be loosed in heaven."

Matthew 16:19

ENGLISH TRANSLATION
BINDING/LOOSING

When I was about 12 years old, my grandfather took me to survey some land that belonged to our family. We spent much of the day out in the woods. He showed me places that my grandmother visited as she was growing up. I saw a tree where she had carved her initials as a child. We found a few discarded hams lying in the leaves – you know, a typical walk through the forest.

Then, as we were reaching the edge of the property, we came upon a barbed-wire fence. I had, of course, seen fences like this on television and in movies, but never up close. I had always been curious about something: does it hurt to touch a barbed-wire fence?

Now, obviously, I knew that the barbs would be sharp. But what about the fence itself?

So I touched it.

And it was electrified.

Before I realized it, volts of electricity were flowing through my hand and up my arm. I quickly yanked back my hand and, thankfully, was unharmed, save for a few hairs left standing up on my hand.

When I think about that moment, though, the impulse to touch that fence, it reminds me of something I've witnessed in countless people throughout my life: people love to test boundaries.

Spend just ten minutes with a toddler, and you will realize that it is hard-wired into our brains to test what is safe and what is unsafe; what is permitted and what is forbidden.

The same was true in Jesus' day, as well.

There was a popular phrase at the time of Jesus that we see in Matthew's gospel. Jesus tells Simon Peter,

"I WILL GIVE YOU THE KEYS OF THE KINGDOM OF HEAVEN; WHATEVER YOU BIND ON EARTH WILL BE BOUND IN HEAVEN, AND WHATEVER YOU LOOSE ON EARTH WILL BE LOOSED IN HEAVEN"

MATTHEW 16:19

The words for binding and loosing are the Hebrew words *asar* and *hitir*. At the time of Jesus, they also referred to things that were forbidden and permitted. For instance, religious leaders would determine which activities were forbidden (bound) on the Sabbath and which ones were permitted (loosed).

So, when Jesus tells Simon Peter that he is giving him the keys to the kingdom, that whatever he binds on earth will be bound in heaven, and whatever he looses on earth will be loosed in heaven, we now have a better sense of what he is saying.

Jesus is telling Simon Peter that he now has the ability to determine what is prohibited and what is permitted for future generations.

When churches began to form around the world, and especially as the gospel spread to non-Jewish populations, there were many questions about what was required and what was not.

Should new Gentile converts be required to observe biblical food laws?
Did they need to return to Jerusalem for major festivals?
Could they still purchase meat, even though it had been sacrificed to false idols?

Many such questions had never even been discussed before. So Jesus made Simon Peter responsible for deciding what was forbidden and what was permitted. In fact, Simon Peter and other leaders ended up doing this when faced with some major questions in Acts 15.

Even today, we still wrestle with this. What parts of scripture are permitted, and which are not? How much of the Old Testament do we have to obey? All? None? Some?

In the end, many of those answers may never be clear to us. So we must continuously look to scripture and the Holy Spirit to help us discern what is *asar* and what is *hitir* … what is required, and what is not.

How does this understanding of *asar* and *hitir* change the way you see Jesus' words to Simon Peter?

_____
_____
_____
_____
_____
_____
_____

What commands from the Old Testament do you think we are still "bound" to?

_____
_____
_____
_____
_____
_____
_____
_____

As Christians, how do we determine which commandments from the Old Testament we are still bound to?

_____
_____
_____
_____
_____
_____
_____

RELATED SCRIPTURES TO STUDY

MATTHEW 18:18

KALOT & CHAMUROT

KAW-LOTE' & KHAW-MOO-ROTE'

חמורות | קלות

"Therefore anyone who sets aside one of the *least of these* commands and teaches others accordingly will be called least in the kingdom of heaven, but whoever practices and teaches these commands will be called great in the kingdom of heaven."

Matthew 5:19

ENGLISH TRANSLATION
LIGHTWEIGHT/SERIOUS

29 | KALOT & CHAMUROT

I have loved baseball for as long as I can remember. Some of my earliest memories involve throwing the baseball with my grandfather, driving to the field early on Saturday mornings for practice, and eating oatmeal pies and fudge rounds provided by parents at the end of each game.

The problem is, I wasn't very good at baseball. When I watch videos of myself playing at an early age, I look like a newborn giraffe who doesn't know how to walk yet. I was totally uncoordinated and incredibly awkward.

So, while I never excelled at baseball, I did become very good at something related to it: collecting baseball cards.

To this day, I still love opening a pack of baseball cards, learning about the players, and sorting them into pages and binders.

One of the things that I especially liked to do was rank my cards. I would create piles of cards, sorted from best to worst. Sometimes my decision was based on the value of the card. At other times, it was simply subjective.

I think sorting and ranking things is something all of us do to some degree, even if we don't realize it.

We will rank our favorite restaurants, television shows, and worship songs. We will even sometimes rank sin.

Have you ever had a conversation like that, one where you discuss with others which sins are the worst and which are less bad?

It may surprise you to know, though, that this debate is nothing new. People have been forming moral hierarchies for millennia. And at the time of Jesus, rather than ranking sins, they ranked commandments.

In fact, this debate led to the formation of two Hebrew idioms that appear in the gospels.

In Hebrew, the word *kalot* means "lightweight." The word *chamurot* means "serious."

101

Sometime before the first century, these two words developed into idioms outlining a hierarchy of biblical commands. Mitzvot *kalot* referred to a light commandment. And mitzvot *chamurot* referred to a heavy commandment. This meant that mitzvot *kalot* were commandments that were less important, and mitzvot *chamurot* were more important.

With this in mind, suddenly, Jesus' words at the beginning of the Sermon on the Mount take on a different meaning. Jesus says that anyone who sets aside "one of the least of these commands" and teaches others to do the same will be least in the Kingdom of God.

Most likely, Jesus is using the phrase mitzvot *kalot*. He's telling people not to dismiss what people have defined as the less important commandments.

This is further illustrated in what Jesus says next. He begins to highlight light and heavy commandments, telling his followers to be sure to obey even the light commandments.

Jesus says, don't just refrain from murder; also refrain from angry and harmful actions towards your neighbor.
Don't just refrain from adultery; also refrain from lust.
Don't just respond proportionally through the practice of eye for an eye; refrain from any retribution against someone who has wronged you.

In other words, just like we shouldn't try to rank sin, we shouldn't rank God's commands. Everything we see in scripture is the word of God. And if we can't honor the light commandments, we can't truly honor any of them.

Have you ever ranked sin? What sins did you say were truly terrible? Which ones did you say were less bad?	Are there commandments in scripture that you follow more than others?	What are some "light" commandments that are important for us to follow?
_____	_____	_____
_____	_____	_____
_____	_____	_____
_____	_____	_____
_____	_____	_____
_____	_____	_____
_____	_____	_____
_____	_____	_____

OTHER PASSAGES TO STUDY

From the Talmud:

"The child;" these are people who are devoid of mitzvot, who will behave insolently toward one who is as filled with mitzvot as a pomegranate. "And the base against the honorable;" this means that one for whom *major* transgressions are like *minor* ones in his mind will come and behave insolently with one for whom even minor transgressions are like major ones in his mind" (Chigigah 14a:14).

EGO EIMI

EG-O' I-MEE'

ἐγώ εἰμί

"Very truly," Jesus answered,
"before Abraham was born, *I Am.*"

John 8:58

What is your name?

This is one of the first questions we ask someone we are meeting for the first time. By knowing a person's name, we know how to refer to them. We hold a piece of their identity in our mouths.

And this simple act runs deep, doesn't it?

Our names matter to us. We feel valued when someone refers to us by our name rather they saying "hey, buddy" or "thanks, sport." General terms feel impersonal and unimportant. But our name means something.

When someone hears our name, we hope that they hear more than a mere word. We hope that they understand that this cognomen is a reference to our very identity, everything that matters about us: our character, our personality, our dreams, and even our struggles.

This is why names are so important in the Bible. Names are more than mere words. Names say something about a person at a much deeper level.

Abraham means "exalted father."
David means "beloved."
Ichabod means "God's glory has left Israel." (Yikes!)

So, we should pay attention to the various names given to Jesus, especially when he uses certain names to describe himself.

In fact, there is one particular phrase that Jesus uses often, but is very easy to overlook. Again and again, Jesus refers to himself using the phrase *ego eimi*, which translates "I Am." But this phrase is more than merely a first-person singular verb.

You see, long before Jesus came to earth, a prophet named Moses encountered God's presence at a burning bush that was not being consumed. God was making a promise to Moses that God would free the Israelite people from slavery in Egypt. And before Moses left to share this message with the Israelite people, he asked the Lord a very basic question:

What is your name? (In other words, Who shall I say has sent me?)

And do you know what God said?

In the Septuagint, which is the Greek translation of the Old Testament that arose several hundred years before Jesus, God's reply is "*ego eimi*."

I Am.

When Jesus uses this phrase to refer to himself, like when he says,

"VERY TRULY...BEFORE ABRAHAM WAS BORN, I AM"

JOHN 8:58

people knew exactly what he meant.

He wasn't accidentally using the same name God gave to Moses.
He was identifying himself as "I Am."
He was claiming to be God.

Often, people will say that Jesus never makes claims of divinity in scripture. But such an argument makes little sense when considering how often the phrase *ego eimi* appears in the gospels. Jesus uses this phrase more than 50 times, just in John's gospel alone.

It isn't an accident. It isn't a coincidence. It isn't random.

The gospels make a profound point: God has walked among us, shared our humanity, died for our sins, and risen so that we might have new life.

They each understand this. They know his identity. Jesus is "I Am."

Use a resource like blueletterbible.org or Logos to search for the phrase ego eimi. How does your new understanding of this term impact the way you interpret these passages?	What are some other instances in scripture where Jesus claims to be God?	Why is this truth so important to our beliefs as Christians?

RELATED SCRIPTURES TO STUDY

EXODUS 3:14   JOHN 14:6

AFTERWORD

OF ALL THE LESSONS I HAVE LEARNED THROUGH MY STUDIES OVER THE PAST DECADE, I BELIEVE THAT THE *SHEMA* IS MY FAVORITE.

For most of my life, I thought that these were words Jesus made up when he issued forth the Great Commandment. I thought that when Jesus said the word *Shema*, he was just trying to get our attention, to invite us to listen.

I had no idea how much meaning there was still left to uncover.

I think what matters most to me about the *Shema* is how much it mattered to Jesus. There is something amazing in knowing that you are praying a prayer that Jesus himself prayed every day of his life. It is a prayer that was central to his identity and the identity of his people.

To understand the *Shema* is to begin to understand the Israelite people. And the better we understand the Israelite people, the better we can understand Jesus.

But there's more, isn't there?

Because in the *Shema* we also see an outline for what our relationship with Jesus should look like. When we understand words like *lev*, *nephesh*, and *m'eod* as the Israelite people understood them, as Jesus understood them, we can clearly understand not only what Jesus is asking of us, but what he did for us.

That he is our ultimate example of *agape*.

That it from his very *lev* came the words that brought us into being.

That he took on flesh and devoted his *nephesh* to preparing us to receive his Kingdom and salvation.

And that he poured out every last ounce of his *m'eod* in sacrifice for us, that we might have new life through him.

When we move *Beyond the Words*, we find that alll of scripture, even the parts we don't understand, even the things we didn't notice – all of it – has been proclaiming this same message of how much God loves us and how much we are invited to love God.

I pray that you know this love. May you understand just how much God loves you and how God proved this through Jesus. May you return that love, fully surrendering yourself to Jesus, allowing him to be your Lord and your Savior. And may you continue to search God's Word for this good news, that God might not only continue to bless you through the gospel but that God might also use you to spread this hope to others, that all might worship Jesus and witness God's Kingdom here on earth as it is in heaven.

God bless!

Brandon Robbins

READING PLAN REFLECTION QUESTIONS

ONE PER DAY

☐ **DAY 1 // YADA = KNOW**

Jeremiah 24:7 | Exodus 1:8 | Isaiah 12:5 | Ezekiel 20:39-44

What one step can you take today to deepen your relationship with the Lord?

☐ **DAY 2 // SHEMA = HEAR & OBEY**

Deuteronomy 6:4-5 | Genesis 27:8 | Isaiah 1:10 | Mark 4:9

Where have you been hearing God speak, and now you need to obey?

☐ **DAY 3 // AGAPE = LOVE**

1 Corinthians 13:4-7 | John 15:13 | 2 Corinthians 5:14 | 1 John 4:8

To whom can you show agape love today?

☐ **DAY 4 // LEV = HEART**

Psalm 9:1 | Exodus 4:21 | Proverbs 12:25 | Matthew 6:21

What would it look like if you loved God with all of your "heart" (thoughts)?

☐ **DAY 5 // NEPHESH = SOUL**

1 Kings 8:48-49 | Psalm 116:7 | Jeremiah 6:16

What would it look like if you loved God with all of your "soul" (every part of your life)?

☐ **DAY 6 // M'EOD = STRENGTH**

Deuteronomy 6:5 | 1 Samuel 28:20

What would it look like if you loved God with all of your "strength" (every ounce of energy you've got)?

☐ DAY 7 // AVAD = SERVE

Exodus 8:1 | Joshua 24:31 | Job 21:15 | Jeremiah 5:19

What are some ways you can begin to "serve" God while you "worship"?

☐ DAY 8 // KAYEM & VATEL = FULFILL & ABOLISH

Matthew 5:17 | Mark 7:10-13

Can you think of a scripture that at one point you "abolished" (misinterpreted) that you can now "fulfill" (interpret correctly)?

☐ DAY 9 // LECH ACHARAI = FOLLOW ME

Mark 1:16-17 | Matthew 9:9 | Luke 18:18-30

How does this phrase change the way you understand what it means to "follow" Jesus?

☐ DAY 10 // RABBI = TEACHER

John 1:38 | Matthew 23:1-12 | John 3:2

What do you need to surrender in your life in order for Jesus to truly be your "*rabbi*"?

☐ DAY 11 // MATHETES = DISCIPLE

Matthew 28:19-20 | Matthew 13:52 | Acts 14:21

How would you explain to others what it means to be a "disciple" of Jesus?

☐ DAY 12 // TORAH = LAW & INSTRUCTION

Matthew 5:17 | Exodus 24:12 | Psalm 1:2 | Proverbs 7:2

How has your understanding of Old Testament "law" changed?

☐ DAY 13 // SANE & MISEO = HATE

Luke 14:26 | Exodus 20:5 | Matthew 6:24

How could your calendar better reflect the things that you "love" and "hate"?

☐ DAY 14 // BEN = SON

Matthew 1:1 | Genesis 10 | Numbers 1:1-16 | Luke 3:21-38

How are Jesus' ancestors a reflection of who he will be and what he will do?

☐ DAY 15 // MAKARIOS = BLESSED

Matthew 5:3 | Luke 14:12-15 | James 1:12 | Revelation 14:13

How does this understanding of "blessed" change the way you read the Beatitudes?

☐ DAY 16 // MAGOI = MAGI

Matthew 2:2 | Acts 13:58

What does it tell us about Jesus that God sent Gentiles from afar to come and worship him?

☐ DAY 17 // YIRAH = FEAR

Isaiah 11:3 | Genesis 20:11 | Psalm 34:11 | Ephesians 5:21

How has this new understanding of the word *yirah* changed the way you interpret what it means to "fear" God?

☐ DAY 18 // YESHUA = GOD SAVES

Matthew 1:21 | Zechariah 3

How has Jesus brought salvation to your life and the world around you?

☐ DAY 19 // MASHIACH & CHRISTOS = ANOINTED ONE

Mark 1:1 | Daniel 9:25-26 | Matthew 24:5,23 | Acts 18:28

How are you relying upon Jesus to be your Messiah?
What other things in your life are you tempted to trust in?

☐ DAY 20 // SHAYM = NAME

Exodus 20:7 | Isaiah 25:1 | Micah 6:9 | John 14:14

How willl this word change the way you pray in the "name" of Jesus?

☐ DAY 21 // SHALOM = PEACE

Judges 6:23-24 | Genesis 28:20-21 | Psalm 72:3 | Isaiah 38:17

What is one way that you can share *shalom* with someone today?

☐ DAY 22 // AION = AGE

Matthew 12:23 | Matthew 13:49 | 1 Timothy 6:19 | Titus 2:12

What hopes do these scriptures give you for the "age" to come?

☐ DAY 23 // HAGAH = MEDITATE

Joshua 1:8 | Isaiah 31:4 | Isaiah 38:14 | Isaiah 59:11

How could *hagah* change the way you pray and spend time with the Lord?

☐ DAY 24 // AYIN TOVAH & AYIN RA'AH = GOOD EYE & BAD EYE

Matthew 6:22-23 | Deuteronomy 15:9 | Proverbs 22:9

What are some ways in which God is challenging you to have a "good eye"?

☐ DAY 25 // BARAK = BLESS

Psalm 34:1 | Job 2:9 | Psalm 103:2 | Psalm 135:19

What would it look like for you to "bless" God at each meal?

☐ DAY 26 // AMEN = I AGREE

1 Chronicles 16:36 | Deuteronomy 27:15-26 | Isaiah 65:16 | Jeremiah 11:5

How does this word change the way you think about ending your prayers?

☐ DAY 27 // RAV = MASTER

1 Kings 25:12 | Genesis 25:23 | Proverbs 28:16 | Jeremiah 39:13

In what ways do you need to surrender and serve Jesus?

☐ DAY 28 // ASAR & HITIR = BINDING & LOOSING

Matthew 16:19 | Matthew 18:18 | Acts 15:1-21

How did the early church handle the responsibility of binding and loosing the law? How should we?

☐ DAY 29 // KALOT & CHAMUROT = LIGHTWEIGHT & SERIOUS

Matthew 5:19

What are some "light" commandments that are easy for us to overlook or ignore?

☐ DAY 30 // EGO EIMI = I AM

John 8:58 | Exodus 3:14 | John 14:6

What difference does it make to our faith that Jesus was fully God and fully human?

FREE BONUS TEACHING!

Thank you so much for purchasing this *"Beyond the Words"* devotional. To show my gratitude, I'd like to share with you five more words that will change the way you read the Bible. Just follow the link below that will take you a page where you can access this exclusive teaching, just for those who have purchased the devotional!

scan code or visit

brandonrobbinsministry.com/devotionalbonus

113

ABOUT THE AUTHOR

BRANDON ROBBINS

Brandon Robbins is a United Methodist pastor and YouTube content creator. His YouTube channel has more than 125,000 subscribers and 7 million views. He is a *#girldad* with two beautiful daughters and an amazing wife, LeeAnn. When he isn't leading his church or making videos, he loves to read, travel, and search for the world's best hot sauce!

To check out Brandon's YouTube videos and other resources, scan the code or visit
brandonrobbinsministry.com

ACKNOWLEDGEMENTS

I never thought that I would have the opportunity to reach this many people. Three years ago, when I began my YouTube channel, I considered myself lucky to get 50 views on a video, most of whom were probably my mom clicking the "refresh" button. So each day, I give thanks to the Lord for the doors that have opened and the gift that this ministry has become in my life. I believe the Good News of Jesus is the greatest message that anyone can hear. And it is he who deserves all the praise!

I would also like to thank **my wife** for all of her support, both while I have been working on this devotional, and since my ministry began. Many times, she has seen me sitting in front of the computer late at night, working on a chapter or editing a video. She has stood by my side both in moments of elation and frustration. Never has she wavered. LeeAnn, I cherish you. And I couldn't do this without you.

To my beautiful daughters: you are the greatest gift that God has ever given me and your mother. Everything else could disappear tomorrow, but our lives would still be filled with joy because we have you. Thank you for the cuddles on a hard day that wipe away the stress of work, the invitations to play that remind me never to get lost in a task, and for simply bringing such joy and love into our lives each day.

To my parents, my sister, and my extended family: without you, I would not know Jesus. From the Bible stories you would tell me as a child to your consistent presence in church, you helped establish the foundation of my faith. Everything God has done since has been a result of the work God did through you so early on. You have made this ministry possible in ways you will never know.

To my church: thank you for the honor of being your pastor. You bring scripture to life, showing so many what it looks like to be the body of Christ today. Through you, our community knows what it is to be loved by Jesus and invited into a relationship with him. You are truly people who care about people, and I look forward to the work God still has yet to do through us.

To **Frances McHugh**: one of the greatest moments in my life was when God brought you and Lonnie to serve with us at that soup kitchen. It has truly been an honor to serve God alongside you since that day, and to call you friend. You have been part of this ministry since before it was even really a ministry – back when it was just an idea. And I think it's safe to say the vision for this book never would have come to life without your help. **Thank you!**

To **Jennifer Crenshaw**: you have truly been a gift from the Lord. Your patience, generosity, and considerable time spent helping to edit this devotional have truly made it better. It is an even greater blessing to others because of your help and support. I don't know how to thank you enough!

SOURCES

As I created this devotional, I drew upon things I've learned from a variety of sources over the years. Most insights are found in multiple sources. The list below are books that I have found especially helpful and would recommend to those who desire to know more about the world of Jesus, the geography of the Holy Land, and the languages of the Bible.

BOOKS

Jesus Through Middle Eastern Eyes: Cultural Studies in the Gospels
Kenneth E. Bailey, 2008

Listening to the Language of the Bible: Hearing It Through Jesus' Ears
Lois Tverberg with Bruce Okkema, 2004

Misreading Scripture with Western Eyes: Removing Cultural Blinders to Better Understand the Bible
E. Randolph Richards & Brandon J. O'Brien, 2012

New Light on the Difficult Words of Jesus: Insights from His Jewish Context
David Bivin, 2005

Sitting at the Feet of Rabbi Jesus: How the Jewishness of Jesus Can Transform Your Faith
Ann Spangler & Lois Tverberg, 2018

Walking in the Dust of Rabbi Jesus: How the Jewish Words of Jesus Can Change Your Life
Lois Tverberg, 2013

MEDIA

The Chosen, TheChosen.TV
Drama series created, directed, and co-written by American filmmaker Dallas Jenkins.

It is the first-ever multi-season, crowd-funded television series about the life and ministry of Jesus of Nazareth as seen through the eyes of those who knew Him.

2017-present (seven seasons planned).

Rotten Tomatoes: Critics - 100%; Audience - 97%. IMDb: 9.4/10.

Be sure to download the free app.